TRAINING THE
HUNTING
RETRIEVER

Books by Jerome Robinson

The Field & Stream *Deer Hunting Handbook*

Hunt Close!

In the Turkey Woods

Training the Hunting Retriever

TRAINING THE
HUNTING
RETRIEVER

JEROME B. ROBINSON

THE LYONS PRESS

GUILFORD, CONNECTICUT
AN IMPRINT OF THE GLOBE PEQUOT PRESS

Library of Congress Cataloging-in-Publication Data

Robinson, Jerome B.
Training the hunting retriever / Jerome B. Robinson.
p. cm.
Originally published: Canaan, N.H. : J.B. Robinson, 1987.

ISBN 1-55821-936-6 (pb)
1. Retrievers—Training. I. Title.

SF429.R4R63 1999
636.752'735—dc21

99-33157
CIP

Manufactured in the United States of America
First Edition/Fourth Printing

CONTENTS

ACKNOWLEDGEMENTS

This book and the Sports Afield magazine articles from which it grew have been made possible by the generosity and willingness of a long list of professional and amateur retriever trainers who are devoted to perpetuating the excellence of hunting retrievers, to all of them we are indebted.

I am particularly indebted to Tom Paugh, Editor of Sports Afield, who has given me the pleasurable opportunity to travel around the country studying how outstanding sporting dog trainers develop the kind of dogs today's hunters are looking for.

Trainers whose methods have helped shape this book include: Omar Driskill, Jim Dobbs, Paul and Barbara Genthner, David Jones, Ron Mathis, Ed Minnogie, Ron Raynor, Joe Riser, D.L. Walters, Jan White, and others, all of them trainers whose methods have been proven by the excellent hunting retrievers they produce.
— J.B.R.

INTRODUCTION

Here is a different kind of retriever training book. It's not about how I train retrievers — it's better than that. This book is a collection of the most successful training techniques used by some of the best professional hunting retriever trainers in the United States.

As Gundog Editor of Sports Afield magazine it has been my pleasant duty to travel about the country interviewing gundog trainers of all sporting breeds and watching how they work. Almost every trainer with whom I have worked has a special twist, something that person does a little differently than the rest of the pack to achieve an extra high level of success. That's what this book is about.

These are training techniques that have been discovered to improve the performances of retrievers that are actually used for hunting. You'll discover how Omar Driskill trains retrievers to turn their heads with his gun so that they will see which bird he is shooting at and better mark it's fall. You'll learn how Ron Mathis gets retrievers to steady themselves without being forced and how Paul and Barbara Genthner use fencing to get retrievers to handle precisely. David Jones's technique for teaching flushing dogs to

Bringing back the game you shoot in the most efficient manner is what a hunting retriever's life is all about. Every step in your training routine should help prepare your dog to fulfill that role.

quarter at close range is ideal for the trainer who works alone a lot of the time. Jim Dobbs explains how modern variable intensity electronic training collars are used to motivate dogs to respond to commands correctly rather than for punishing dogs when they fail. Joe Riser explains maintenance training. There are easy-to-understand lining drills and handling exercises that will bring out your dog's best performance. This represents how today's successful trainers have simplified traditional methods or discovered more direct routes for gaining canine understanding.

In every respect, this is a book for people who will use their dogs for hunting, "the muddy guys in camoflage," as Omar Driskill calls us. The techniques explained here enable you to train your dog for situations it will encounter on frosty mornings when the ducks are flying and the shooting is fast and your mind is on the ducks instead of the dog.

In this book we're training for the real thing.

(1)

The Hunting Retriever Movement

We have entered the era of the Hunting Retriever. At no point in the history of the retriever breeds has so much energy and knowledge been assembled in an effort to realistically evaluate the dogs actually used to bring back the game we shoot.

The Hunting Retriever Club, Inc. (HRC), the North American Hunting Retriever Association (NAHRA), and hunting retriever tests sanctioned by the American Kennel Club (AKC) have attracted mounting enthusiasm all over the country for the simple reason that they are providing better means of rating the performance of the dogs we use for hunting than any evaluating system which has gone before.

The differences between the new hunting retriever tests and traditional field trials are many — all of them clearly differences which true hunters will appreciate. At Hunting Retriever events handlers and judges wear camoflage clothing, not white jackets, for one thing. And they work the dogs out of real duck blinds and duck boats amidst complete sets of decoys. Multiple shots are fired when the birds fall, just as it happens when you are really hunting. Dogs are tested on their tracking ability and the manner in which they

Hunting Retriever tests are for everyone from all walks of life and financial circumstances and for all dogs that can be trained to bring back game that falls to the gun. There are progressive levels of achievement for dogs and handlers who are just starting out all the way through to tests for highly trained dogs with great experience.

At Hunting Retriever Club tests the handlers wear camoflage and shoot shotguns over their dogs. Gun safety is taught and required of all handlers, just as it should be when hunting.

quarter a field in search of upland game as well as their straight retrieving work. At Hunting Retriever events there is a dedication to making sure every test clearly relates to real hunting situations. Anything that smacks of artificialty is spurned. Sponsoring clubs outdo each other to make Hunting Retriever tests so real that those who enter them come away feeling like they have really been hunting.

But the most important difference between the Hunting Retriever events, whether they are sponsored by HRC, NAHRA or AKC, the dogs are judged against written standards which they either pass or fail rather than competing against each other in an attempt to determine which dog does best.

Dogs that are judged passing at Hunting Retriever events win points towards various rankings which describe the level of ability they have achieved. Judging the dogs against defined standards rather than against each other means that many dogs "win" at each Hunting Retriever event, instead of having only one "winner" and all the rest culled out, as happens in traditional field trials.

The lack of competition between dogs and handlers at Hunting

Retriever events makes for a much more friendly atmosphere in which everyone shares training tips and honestly wishes his neighbor a good day. "We're here for the betterment of all the dogs, not to try to beat each other," they tell you at Hunting Retriever events.

The great advantage of this kind of testing becomes apparent when you understand that head to head competition has pushed the level of performance at field trials so far beyond the needs of real hunters that they have become a different game. The ultra-sophisticated tests at licensed field trials today don't recognize the value of honest hunting retrievers; they are geared for dogs of "winning" caliber only, and those that don't win lose.

At Hunting Retriever events, on the other hand, dogs are judged on an escalating scale of achievement and there are rewards at all levels. "We want to make the person with his first dog feel welcome," says Omar Driskill, first president of the Hunting Retriever Club, Inc. "He'll find others at his ability level here and we'll all work together to help him get better performances out of his dog. We

The best hunting retrievers are regular members of the family. Only a small amount of its life is spent actually hunting. Most of the time a hunting retriever is home doing family duty and dreaming about hunting days to come — like the rest of us.

Great effort is made at Hunting Retriever tests to simulate actual hunting situations. Here a handler and his Lab are required to hide under a white sheet in a typical snow goose hunting situation and come out shooting when a white duck is thrown in the distance. The dog must remain steady to shot, then complete the retrieve on command.

hope he'll get interested and continue to train his dog to reach higher and higher levels. We'll all have better dogs in the end."

HRC, NAHRA and the AKC Hunting Retriever tests are all devoted to making the low level entrant welcome and helping him and his dog grow in training achievement. These are events where it doesn't matter how much money you have or how much you paid to have your dog trained. Pros and amateurs enter the same events and their dogs are judged according to their ability to pass the tests without having to outdo one another to "win". Hunters can understand these tests and see why it's important for the dogs to attain higher levels of training.

"Hell, duck season only lasts a couple of months, but I can play this game all year," one typical HRC member explained. "It gives you something to train for all year so your dog is at it's best when the real hunting season comes around."

To find out when HRC, NAHRA or AKC Hunting Retriever

Just like the real thing! At Hunting Retriever tests camoflaged handlers shoot shotguns as shackled ducks are thrown in the distance. Here the dog is worked from a brushed blind in a typical riverbottom duck hunting setup.

events are scheduled in your area, write: Hunting Retriever Club, Inc., 100 East Killgore Rd., Kalamazoo, MI 49001-5598; North American Hunting Retriever Assn., P.O. Box 154, Swanton, VT., 05488; and The American Kennel Club, 51 Madison Ave., New York, N.Y. 10010.

(2)

How To Pick A Hunting Retriever Pup

The pup you choose to be your gundog should be the product of a thoughtful search and process of selection. Your pup will probably be with you for a dozen years or so, your companion at home and a representative of your family wherever he goes. He'll be seen by others as an extension of yourself and his triumphs (or his embarrassing performances) will be yours as well. In selecting your puppy you are making a decision that you will have to live with for a long, long time, for the average gundog buyer tends to stick with the dog he has and keep hoping and training towards better achievements as the years go on rather than trading off the dogs that don't work out and buying new and hopefully better ones.

People will tell you that there's nothing to picking a puppy; you just reach in and grab, and in one sense they are right since no one can tell at seven weeks exactly what a pup will grow up to be. But I would advise you not to do your reaching and grabbing until you have made sure that the pups you are grabbing among are all likely to fill your requirements.

Before you start looking for puppies be absolutely sure that you know which breed you want. Become knowledgeable about the

Pick a pup from parents that look and behave the way you want your hunting retriever to.

looks, style and general application of the various gundog breeds and settle on the one that appeals to you the most. If you know individual gundogs that are pleasing to your eye and have the temperment and personality and manner that appeal to you, then that's the breed for you. Now start looking for individuals within that breed that are most likely to produce pups of equal caliber.

Don't ever consider buying a puppy by mail order from a kennel you have never visited, operated by a man you've never met who is breeding dogs you've never laid eyes on. To get the kind of pup you want, you've got to be sure that the pup's parents have the traits and looks that you admire, and the only way to be sure of that is to see the dogs work. Once you've settled on the breed you want, track down responsible breeders in areas where you can visit their kennels and see what they have. Be sure that the kennel you choose has a reputation for producing good gundogs, not show dogs. Breeders of good gun dogs are usually known to Hunting Retriever clubs, hunting preserve operators, fish and game department personnel, newspaper outdoor columnists — these are people who might be able to tip you off to a good local line of gundogs. Check advertisements in local and regional outdoor publications and in the publications of the Hunting Retriever Association listed in Chapter 1. A good gundog has an intelligent manner, takes training without difficulty and handles easily in the field. Be sure that the pup you choose comes from parents who exhibit those traits as well as a strong hunting desire and a good nose. The man with good dogs will be glad to show you his dogs work.

Don't buy a pup from any litter unless both parents are certified by the Orthopedic Foundation for Animals as being free of hip dysplasia. Ask to see the O.F.A. certificate for each parent.

Hip dysplasia is a hereditary disease which causes mature dogs to have varying degrees of hip joint malformation which prevents hunting dogs from developing their full potential. Hip dysplasia is particularly common among the retriever breeds and must be avoided. Freedom from hip dysplasia can only be certified in dogs more than two years old. The disease does not show up on X-rays of very young pups, therefore it is important to be assured that both parents of the litter are dysplasia-free.

Alright, say you have settled on the breed you want and found a breeder whose dogs you like. Once a litter of pups is produced you're ready to pay your money and make your choice, but wait a minute, there's still some narrowing down to do before you reach in and make your grab.

Do you want a male or female? You may be able to eliminate half the litter over that decision. Generally it's true that males are a little bolder and able to take tougher training methods, but I'd say the real difference is simply that females come in heat twice a year and males don't. It's not fun having a female that comes in heat in hunting season, you've got to work her alone and your friends who run male dogs will blame their dog's mistakes on the bitch in heat whenever they screw up if your dog is around. On the other hand, females are extra affectionate, generally handle with less effort, and if the dog turns out to be what you want, you'll be able to breed her and continue her line with a youngster, whereas a man with a good but unknown male gundog may have difficulty finding someone with a good female who is willing to take a chance on an unproven stud.

Actually, the vast majority of females come in heat in August and February when most hunting seasons are closed. Medications are

[9]

also available from veterinarians to delay the heat cycle for up to two months.

When picking a gundog puppy you'll do best to choose one from a spring-born litter. Pups born in March, April or May can be taught during summer to walk on a leash, come when they are called and stop what they are doing when you holler "no". When autumn arrives they will be old enough to be given some actual hunting experience and can become exceptional performers in their second autumn. Spring-born pups get one more hunting season out of life than pups born in the fall. Since most breeders produce the majority of their pups in the spring for this reason, you will have a wider choice of pups to choose from in the spring than at any other time.

Scientific studies made by Dr. Paul Scott in Maine a decade ago proved that the most advantageous time to pick a pup is when the pup is seven weeks old. At that point in a puppy's development it's brain has achieved its full form and is lacking only experience to make it establish patterns which will dictate the dog's natural habits for the rest of its life. A seven week old puppy is ready to learn and form relationships, and the earliest relationships and habits that are imprinted will govern that dog's personality and trainability. Older pups become more independent of people the longer they are left with their brothers and sisters in a dog-dog, rather than dog-man, relationship. A pup seven weeks old has no further need of its mother and is ready to attach itself to you and accept you as it's idol. Pick your pup and take it home when it is as close to seven weeks as possible and make it a member of the family.

You can't look at a litter of seven week old pups and tell much about the degree of ability each will achieve as it matures. The pup's genetic heredity will determine how good it's nose is going to be, how intelligent it is, it's size and conformation. By assuring yourself that it's parents are dogs you like you have done about all you can to hedge your bet when you make the gamble and choose your pup.

Obviously, any pups that are noticeably shy, frightened, listless or dull should be removed, leaving you with only the happy, healthy, smart looking pups of the sex from which you want to choose.

If the smallest pup in the litter is among those still in the running, look it over carefully. If it is simply a smaller rendition of the others in the litter and exhibits no physical or mental handicaps then that

[10]

pup can be considered simply "the little guy" and could well be your choice. The fact that he's the smallest at this age has nothing to do with how large he may become. If the smallest pup is a true "runt," you'll notice some physical or mental irregularity and common sense will tell you to cancel that one from your prospects.

Arrange to see the puppies when they are being fed. Physical quirks are likeliest to show up then. A healthy pup eats eagerly, has clear eyes and no discharge from eyes or nose, has a firm covering of flesh, not bony hips and ribs, and he's happy and robust, not spooky. A thin pot-bellied pup probably has worms. One with running eyes or a runny nose may have distemper; if there seems to be a question about this, ask the owner to take the pup's temperature and look at the reading yourself. 101.5 degrees is normal, with anything between 101 and 102 being acceptable. Beware of the kennel owner who refuses to take a pup's temperature or claims not to have a thermometer. Anyone who raises puppies without a means of taking temperatures is exhibiting either ignorance or carelessness.

After the pups have finished eating, take your remaining candidates out of the kennel one at a time. In the yard, away from the peer influence of their littermates, young pups reveal a bit more about their underlying natures. Walk away. Does the puppy romp along with you or does it go off by itself not giving a hoot about you? He may grow into that kind of dog as he matures. Is he interested in new things like leaves and sticks and new smells? Does he investigate these new curiousities or seem to fear them? You want the brave little investigator not the timid one. Squat down on your heels and clap your hands lightly. Does the pup come running to you or shy away? Keep your eye on the one that comes eagerly.

Probably your choice has been made for you by this time as one pup or another reacts in a way that eliminates him from your choices. If not, if you still have several pups that pass all the tests and meet your requirements, that's a good time to just close your eyes and grab one. But if one pup is endearing in some special way that even you can't describe, you better play your hunch and put your money on him.

Before you leave with your new pup, the owners should provide you with a copy of his health record showing what shots he has had and whether or not he has been wormed. If your pup is in good condition, you'll do well to keep him on the same diet, so write down what he has become accustomed to eating and stick with that. The owner should also give you a copy of the litter registration certificate and an application for individual registration of your pup.

If you have done your homework before choosing your puppy, you will have assured yourself that your pup comes from a litter produced from a line of dogs with the characteristics that please you. You will be buying from a breeder you have reason to trust. The pups you choose among will be healthy, robust and friendly and will show no signs of physical or mental handicap and their parents will be the same. With those assurances you needn't worry about whether or not you have chosen the "best" pup in the litter. Take the one you like the most — he'll be the best one for you.

(3)

The Importance of Knowing What's Right

Successful dog training depends on your ability to show your dog what is right. Unfortunately, one of the primary mistakes trainers make is to punish dogs for behaving the wrong way without making the dog understand what the right way is. Too many dogs are chronic misbehavers because they have been punished and yelled at so much that they accept this abuse as a normal part of life and learn only to try and avoid training sessions, rather than discovering that there is a right way to do things that cancels out all the commotion.

Looking through the catalogs of dog training aids you see advertised shock collars, electric prods, spike collars, choke collars, whips, sling shots, pellet guns, and the inference is that the tools of punishment are the secrets of successful training. If amateur trainers would spend less time thinking that their dogs would be better if they had this or that training gadget, and would think more about meaningful methods of showing their dogs what is right, there would be a lot of better dogs around.

I am often impressed by the high degree of training that is achieved by people who own house dogs and have never read or heard a single thing about how to train a dog. They simply train by

Keep lessons simple. Make it easy for the dog to understand what is happening and what he is supposed to do. Praise him when he does it right.

example. The old man whose dog goes to the corner store and brings back a newspaper every day was not taught to do that with electric shocks, or whips or spike collars. Instead, the dog grew to love and trust his master because he was fairly treated and well cared for. The dog learned the man's habits and, as good dogs do, he pitched in and tried to help. For this he was rewarded with appreciation so he knew helping with the paper was right and soon he knew the routine well enough to do it on his own.

The little old lady whose housepet sits quietly in the car and does not leap out even though the windows are left open was not taught this degree of staunchness with a checkcord or an electric cattle prod. Nobody stung him with a slingshot when he attempted to leap out. Instead the little old lady had taught her dog to sit by gently pushing him down and repeating the command and then patting the pup when he began to sit on command without being pushed down. She taught him then to stay simply saying "ah-ah" in a cautionary tone when the pup tried to move from his sitting position. When he stayed where he was she said "good boy," in a tone he had grown to know meant he was doing the right thing. Once he understood that the word "stay" meant he was not to move, he knew that staying was right and he would stay wherever she told him to, whether it was in the house or in the car.

Some of the wisest and most companionable dogs around are farm dogs that have never had a lick of formal training or harsh punishment. Yet, they will ride in the back of an open truck without leaping out, they know what come, sit, no and heel, mean and many of them will hunt whatever track you put them on and retrieve anything that is thrown for them or shot in their presence. They learned what is right simply by being encouraged and praised when they did something that pleased their master and verbally scolded when they did something that was considered wrong.

Dogs learn to copy the people who have the most to do with them. If you are fair with your dog and show him by example what you want him to do, he'll try to copy you, watch and see. But if you are so intent on applying a training method that you only punish and never teach, the dog will be confused and scared. He doesn't know what is right. It seems to him that everything he does gets him in trouble. Rather than reason out some alternative behavior which actually might be what you want him to do, he'll simply give up and want to get away

Successful dog training depends on your ability to show your dog what is right.

or stubbornly refuse to do anything at all.

One of the main reasons why professional trainers want to have a dog in their kennels for a minimum of several months is that they have to establish a good relationship with the dog before they can train effectively. A dog has to like his trainer and want to please him before the trainer can get the dog's best performance out of him. That means that the pro needs time to demonstrate to the dog that he is fair as well as firm. Then when he trains he makes sure that the dog knows there is always a right way. Not until the dog shows he understands what the right way is does a good pro punish him for misbehavior.

It's important to remember that the professional trainer must often overcome negative behavior that a dog's owners allowed to become habit before he can begin to teach the dog new things. And the pro is usually expected to get the job done in a minimum of time. To accomplish all this the pro resorts to harsher training methods than need ever be employed by the man who raises a dog from puppyhood and has every day of the pup's life to show him what is right as well as what is wrong.

I once watched a knowledgeable professional trying to speed up a young retriever's delivery. The dog had come to him from an amateur trainer who had been leaning hard on the dog without success. The dog had been stung, shocked, pelleted and whipped for slowing down when it was completing a retrieve and none of these punishments had speeded him up. The dog still raced out, scooped up the bird and then dawdled on the way back.

"This dog has been punished so much he thinks everything he does is wrong," the pro explained. "The one thing his owner hasn't tried is praise. Watch this."

The dog was sent for a dummy and, typically, he picked it up fast and then slowed to a trot and finally a walk on the return. The trainer got down on one knee. "Good boy," he called gently. "Good boy."

You could almost see the dog smile. His whole attitude became refreshed and he picked up his pace and came eagerly towards the trainer.

"He's not speedy yet, but we'll get there," the trainer said. "What that dog needs is to know that coming back fast is good. He's been punished so many times while he was returning with a bird that he thinks you get hurt when you're bringing a bird back. He just needs to know what's right."

When you are training ask yourself what you have done to show him how to do right. Instead of nagging him or getting rough with him for behavior you don't want, how about trying a positive approach with him next time. Try sweetening him up before a lesson. Play with him, pat him, tell him he's good. Get him on your side before you start the lesson. Now try something easy, something you know he'll do right and when he does it, praise the hell out of him. Once you've got him really liking you, move on to your problem area and praise him if he does *anything* right.

In repeated examples, show him what the right way is and make sure he knows you like it when he does the right thing. Then if the time comes when punishment is unavoidable, the dog will have a fair basis from which to make a choice.

Punishment is a necessary part of training, but too often it is overdone. Usually a dog with normal intelligence that is consistently shown what is right and what is wrong in each situation will learn to do basic things right with a minimum of harsh discipline.

(4)

Keys To Successful Dog Training

A man's ability to train a dog is determined by the degree to which he possesses four personal qualities, *timing, consistency, patience,* and *voice control.* It doesn't matter whether you are training a gun dog or a housepet, a wolfhound or a chihuahua, the man who possesses those qualities in high degree will get the job done, and the man in whom those qualities are lacking may wind up feeling like a basket case.

Dog training is not a matter of tricks. Good dog trainers have no secret methods; they train according to logical teaching sequences. The difference is that the good trainer has a highly developed sense of *timing;* he knows when to punish and when not to, when to advance to the next training step and when to drop back. The experienced trainer is a model of *consistency,* and the dogs he trains learn that certain responses to commands always bring him pleasure, while other responses bring trouble. Of course, he's *patient.* Dog training is a matter of repetition. It can be boring to both trainer and the dog. Nevertheless, patient application is what trains the dog. Every good dog trainer has exceptional *voice control.* He doesn't bellow and shout commands, he's calm and quiet, using the tone of his voice, not the volume, to elicit responses.

These four personal qualities, timing, consistency, patience and voice control are the keys to successful dog training. Here's how to develop them in yourself.

Timing

Timing is a matter of knowing when to crack down on a dog and when to ease up. It comes from experience, to be sure, but you can develop your sense of timing faster if you are aware of its importance and think in terms of timing when you are training.

The great professional trainers all have wonderful timing. They do things with dogs that the rest of us would think were strictly taboo. For example, nationally famous retriever trainer Joe Riser sometimes purposely throws away the rules and encourages his dogs to break, bark, chase each other and generally cut-up.

Normally, Joe Riser's retrievers are perfectly mannered; they don't bark in the kennel, they automatically walk at heel when brought out of the truck, and during training sessions a group of them sit in a line without restraint as each one is called by name to come forward and go through his lessons while the others watch. You can't imagine more rigid adherence to the rules.

But every once in a while Joe throws open the doors of the truck and, whooping like a dancing Indian, begins flinging training dummies in every direction, shouting, "Cut loose! School's out! Let 'er go!" He creates a frenzy of canine free-thinking. A dozen dogs will jump into the pond, half drowning each other in the mad scramble to get hold of a dummy. You'll see tugs of war between three dogs trying to retrieve the same dummy; there are dogs running aimlessly in and out of the water. For ten or fifteen minutes Joe keeps it up, whirling dummies every which way and letting the dogs break to chase them, sometimes only half completing a retrieve before dropping the dummy to race off after another. You'd never believe that these are highly trained retrievers.

"Instant disorder," Joe calls it. "The most relaxing thing in the world."

He explains that his dogs are under a rigid training routine and occasionally they need a break. They never know when Joe is going to turn a training session into a three-ring circus, and it keeps them on their toes, eager, with their eye on the boss every moment.

Successful dog training requires a sense of timing, consistent methods, personal patience and a firm, not angry, tone.

"Nothing can be all work and no play," Joe says.

Knowing when to let the bars down, that's timing!

Consistency

Consistency is a matter of always being sure that the dog understands what a command means before he is ever punished for disobeying it. Consistency is also necessary in laying out guidelines of behavior which the dog must live within. Once he has been shown what is permissible and what is not, you must be consistent in demonstrating that breaking the rules brings correction and that proper behavior is rewarded with praise and affection.

In the beginning, when you are not fully familiar with the training sequence you've read about and plan to follow, you may find it hard to be consistent in your reactions when the dog does something you don't want him to do forever, but can excuse while he's young.

In general, make this your rule: when he does something which you will some day have to break him from doing, then correct him every time he exhibits that trait regardless of his age. You needn't punish him, just correct him, show him how you want him to behave. Then when he grows up and must be broken from certain habits, he'll have a background of consistent correction to help him comprehend what it is you want him to do.

Patience

No matter how fine you hone your sense of timing or how readily you become consistent, patience will probably be the most difficult quality to acquire.

Dog training demands repetition. It's a matter of showing the dog again and again what a command means and then enforcing it. Day after day you must review the commands the dog already knows, then progress into a new lesson. At times all this repetition becomes boring to both you and the dog and only patience will pull you through.

If you become impatient with a dog and start nagging at him and let your anger get the best of you, your training for that day is done. You're better off putting the dog back in the kennel and postponing the training session until some time when you can be patient with him. You can't expect to successfully teach the dog how to behave at moments when you have lost control over your own reactions. Angry tirades only scare the dog and cause him to question his trust in you. When your dog needs punishment keep your cool and punish him calmly. That way he'll realize that he is being punished for misbehaving. If you become impatient and blow up at him and scare him, he'll forget what it was he did wrong and simpy remember that there are times when you go mad.

[22]

Voice Control

We all know men who bellow at their dogs. "Get in here. . ." "Get over there. . ." They seem to have only one tone of voice (angry) and one volume (loud). Rarely are their dogs any good.

In dog training as in the raising of decent children, it is not what you say, it's how you say it that gets the message through. The best dog trainers have a wide variety of tones of voice they employ in training. By their tone they communicate to the dog that what he is doing pleases them or is just passable performance or will not be permitted to continue. They have a tone of warning which they use when the dog seems about to make an error, one of reassurance to help bolster the dog when he acts timid, an affectionate tone for quiet moments.

They do not shout commands but rather speak them clearly at a volume which the dog can hear easily. Volume increases according to the distance between the dog and the trainer, but it's tone of voice, not volume, that tells the dog whether or not the trainer is pleased with the dog's performance.

It's a matter of saving the heavy artillery for really serious trouble. When the dog intentionally disobeys a command he fully understands the trainer combines an angry tone of voice with an increase in volume, and the effect is very startling to the dog. A dog that has not been shouted at except when he makes a very serious error, is much more impressed by his trainer's loudness than one that is accustomed to being shouted at all the time.

You've undoubtedly seen dogs that are positively awed and immediately humbled by their master's firmly spoken "ah-ah!" and others that go right on doing whatever they feel like despite their master's bulgy-eyed, red-faced swearing and yelling and carrying on.

You can develop good voice control if you concentrate on conveying your feelings through the tone of your voice rather than by loud shouting. You'll find voice control helps make life a lot more pleasant and that it is effective on other than canine members of the family as well.

In dog training you want the end result to be a sociably acceptable, friendly companion with certain specialties. You don't want to create a robot that automatically does what you say and never thinks for himself; therefore you do not exert such force that you obliterate the dog's spirit. But neither do you want to produce a dog so free-willed that he has no understanding of authority.

(5)

How To Use Electronic Training Collars

Electronic dog training has matured to the point where it can be said that today every person who undertakes to train a gundog can benefit by using an electronic training collar. This was not always the case. When electronic training collars first came on the market they were a scourge that when used improperly probably ruined more dogs than they helped. Now that has changed. Today the best electronic training collars have been advanced to a degree that makes them probably the most useful tool a trainer can own.

Here's what has happened:

The early collars were strictly devices for dealing out punishment at a distance. The handler held a radio transmitter and when he pushed the button the dog received a high voltage shock from the receiver attached to its collar. These collars were good for breaking dogs off chasing deer and other bad habits and could be used sparingly in the process of convincing a dog that it could be punished even at long distance when it disobeyed commands. The trouble was that the collars were too "hot" for all but the toughest dogs. A lot of dogs simply refused to do anything for fear of doing something that would cause that awful collar to go off.

Modern electronic training collars have advanced so far that every trainer can benefit by using one. Be sure to choose a model that offers variable intensity and a caution buzzer.

There was another problem with the people who bought the early collars. Too often frustrated trainers tried to get their money's worth by using the collar too much. They wound up with dogs that were afraid to leave their sides. It was too easy for a trainer to lose his temper and "fry the dog" every time the dog did something wrong.

You could tell a "collar dog" the minute you saw one. Head hanging, tail drooping, scared of it's shadow. The early collars were only used successfully by people who fully understood their power and could restrain themselves from overusing them.

Today much better electronic training collars are available and dog training methods are being altered to use the new collars in much more effective ways. Instead of using the electronic collar as a device for meting out remote punishment when the dog does something wrong, the new collars are used to motivate the dog to respond properly.

This different approach is possible because the modern collars, such as the Tri-Tronics avoidance trainers, have two very important features that old fashioned models do not have; variable intensity and a caution buzzer. Those two features are what make modern electronic training collars useful for all trainers.

Variable intensity means that you can adjust the level of shock the collar delivers to suit the requirements of the dog you are training. The rule is that you set the intensity at the level that causes your dog to feel an unpleasant sensation but not so high that it is frightening to the dog. The required intensity varies with each individual dog.

The caution buzzer is a warning. When you press the red *shock button* the dog hears an audible buzz from his collar just before he feels the electronic stimulation. When you press the yellow *caution button* the dog hears the same audible buzz but does not receive the unpleasant sensation. Once he learns to anticipate that the buzz will be followed by a low level shock unless he obeys your command immediately, he will become eager to obey commands in order to *avoid* the shock. This feature enables you to communicate a painless warning to the dog that he must obey.

Two men shoot a released pigeon as one trainer is ready to keep his dog steady with an electronic training collar and another uses a stick to enforce steadiness in her Lab.

Variable intensity enables you to transmit low level stimulation to your dog without actually hurting him and the caution button gives you a means of communicating a reminder to the dog which keeps him eager to respond to commands and assures that he will be paying attention.

For many years the leader in manufacture of electronic training collars has been Tri-Tronics, Inc. of Tucson, Arizona. Tri-Tronics was the first to come out with collars featuring variable intensity and the caution button and has been a leader in teaching the concept of *avoidance training* in which the collars are used to motivate dogs to respond to commands in order to avoid unpleasant electronic stimulation rather than using them for punishing dogs after they do something wrong.

Say you put a rat in a cage which has a hurdle across the middle and an electric grid on one side of the hurdle and a light on the wall. When you press a button the light goes on and a second later the electric grid gives out a shock. In trying to avoid the shock, the rat will jump over the hurdle to the safe side of the cage. After a few of these experiences whenever he sees the light bulb go on he will jump over the hurdle to get on the safe side before the shock occurs. This is the basis of avoidance training. It has been accepted in animal behavior literature ever since Palov noted that dogs would salivate at the sound of a bell once they had been conditioned to understand that the bell always preceded feeding.

Avoidance training is what makes a horse turn it's head when you apply pressure with the bit; the horse turns it's head to stop the pressure and, presto, he's heading in the direction you want him to go.

Avoidance training is based upon understanding that whatever an animal does to turn off an unpleasant sensation will become a permanent response if it is consistently repeated. Before avoidance training can begin you must teach the dog the meaning of the commands you give. These lessons are taught by the traditional methods which appear later in this book. Once the dog has a clear understanding of how he must respond when a command is given, you can use the variable intensity electronic collar to motivate an immediate correct response.

Dogs that are trained in this manner do not exhibit the old "collar dog" fears and dejected nature that are embarrassing visible signs

Instantaneous response to the SIT command or whistle can be attained by fastening an electronic training collar around the dog's loins with the shock points mounted on top of the back. When the command is given the dog receives low intensity electronic stimulation. As it sits the stimulation is stopped. The dog learns it can turn off the stimulation by sitting instantly when ordered to.

of dogs that have learned to fear punishment by electric shock. Instead, avoidance-trained dogs are happy, tail-wagging critters that are confident that there is nothing to be afraid of because they know how to *avoid* electronic stimulation by responding properly to commands. They have been trained using a level of electronic stimulation which does not hurt or frighten them, thanks to the variable intensity feature of good modern collars, and they have learned how to turn the thing off rather than living in dread of a lightning bolt from the sky.

(6)

Starting Right
With Retrievers

Registered Labrador retrievers in the United States now number more than half a million. The breed is the third most popular canine in the country and the Number One sporting breed. However, just as there are more Labs around then ever before, there are also a greater number that fail to make it as hunting dogs.

Paul and Barbara Genthner of Tealbrook Kennels, Monticello, Florida, two of the nations top trainers of retriever gundogs, say that fully a third of the Labs sent to them for training must be returned to their owners because the dogs are unfit for training.

"Twenty years ago ninety percent of the Labs we saw could be trained to make good gundogs," Paul recalled. "But today there are so many Labs being produced for the pet market without regard for hunting and retrieving that a lot of good bloodlines have been diluted."

"That is not to say that all of the washouts fail to become gundogs because of poor breeding alone," the Genthners explain. "Many of the young dogs that are sent to us could have overcome their faults through training if they had been given a better start. Too many are ruined at a young age by owners' mistakes."

According to the Genthners many pups become discouraged about retrieving at a very young age because their owners unwittingly make them believe that retrieving is bad.

A new puppy in the house can be a real pest. He's into everything, dragging out slippers, chewing shoes and furniture, tearing up magazines. In most cases Dad is off at work and Mom and the kids are left with the new dog. If their reaction is to scold the pup, cuff him and snatch away everything he picks up and carries, that pup is being taught at a very vulnerable age that he is not to carry things in his mouth. In many cases an early experience like that is enough to kill the pup's retrieving instinct and render him untrainable for gundog use.

Chances are that when the pup's antics reach an intolerable point the pup will be banished to a kennel and will grow up lacking human contact. By the time he is finally sent to a professional trainer he may be beyond help.

The Genthners suggest that new puppy owners can avoid such

When you have a new retriever pup it is natural to want to see if it has natural retrieving instincts. Use a small paint roller for early retrieves, but don't do much of it. Retrieving training should wait until after the pup has grown its adult teeth, usually at about six months of age.

unfortunate early experiences by starting a pup off right.

"Before a person buys a pup he should have an outdoor kennel and a canine shipping crate of the type used on airplanes," the Genthners advise. "The crate should be kept in a quiet corner of the house where it is out of the way. For short periods of time each day, the pup should be shut up in the crate. At first he will cry about this incarceration, so it may be best to start by closing him up in the crate during times when you will be out of the house for an hour or so. Once he stops fighting the crate he will accept it as his place and will remain quiet when locked in it. He should be provided with a rawhide chew bone as well. Whenever the pup starts chewing on something undesirable, you simply take that object away from him gently and substitute the chew bone without scolding him."

Immediately after the pup drinks or is fed he should be put outside in the kennel so that he establishes the kennel as the only place he moves his bowels or urinates. He should be left in the kennel for a few hours to exercise and get fresh air. When you are ready to have him back in the house open the kennel and call his name and say "Come." He will want to come in the house, so he will obey immediately and will establish an early habit of coming when he is called.

Once in the house you should establish boundaries, a certain room, perhaps with linoleum floors, in which he must stay until he becomes housebroken.

"Don't rough house with him in the house and don't play retrieving games in the house," the Genthners warn. "Playing and rough house are strictly outdoor activities. When he is in the house he should be in his crate, or remaining quiet within the boundaries you define. Once the dog is housebroken you can let him come in other rooms but don't let him get on furniture. Provide him with his own bed on which he can lie near you when he is in the house.

Give him periods of exercise outdoors so that he will be more ready to be quiet when he comes in the house.

It is very important for a pup to have a lot of human contact and socialization. A dog that spends too much time in a kennel and not enough in the house with people, never becomes a comfortable dog to have in the house. These days most gundogs are family pets, too, and need to be raised as companions in the house as well as the duckblind.

[33]

Puppies just have to chew things. You'll be smart to provide your pup with a chewing toy or rawhide bone and hand it to him every time the chewing urge transports him. Otherwise your shoe bill is going to skyrocket.

When to Start Retrieving

As for retrieving, it's natural that a puppy owner will want to assure himself that his pup has retrieving instincts but it is important not to push retrieving too hard too soon.

"Throw a tennis ball or a soft-covered paint roller for a pup and see if he retrieves it once in a while, but once you've seen that a puppy runs out and picks the object up, you really needn't do anything more," Paul says. "If he runs out and picks up something you throw then he has retrieving instincts and can be trained later once he matures a bit."

The Genthners do not recommend beginning retrieving until a dog has lost his baby teeth and replaced them with adult teeth, usually around six or seven months. Not until that age can you really begin retrieving practice in any meaningful way, and there is too much danger of a younger pup becoming bored with retrieving and getting discouraged.

Then, when retrieving work begins, the Genthners recommend

that only dummies, not birds be used.

"Too many owners can't wait to start shooting birds over their dogs," Paul warns. "The trouble is that a young dog trained on birds will not want to work with dummies later. So, if you have a problem, say the pup starts chewing his birds, you have no recourse. On the other hand, if the pup is trained fully on dummies before he is introduced to birds, you can always go back to working with dummies if problems are encountered later. I'd rather see a dog develop good retrieving habits, a soft mouth, nice delivery, with dummies before he is started on birds. Dogs that become good retrievers before they are introduced to birds rarely become hard-mouthed later."

Introduction to Water

Proper introduction to water is very important. "If the water is warm enough to go in with a bathing suit, it's fine for starting pups," says Paul. "Walk along in shallow water letting the pup play along the edge until he gets used to being wet. Then wade in deeper and call him to you. Never pick him up and throw him in or force him in any way. Let him make up his own mind about water. Then throw a small ball for him in shallow water gradually encouraging him in deeper until he finally goes over his head and finds he can swim."

The Genthners have overcome some retriever's water shyness by leaving the dog on a small island about twenty feet from shore as they work other dogs in the water nearby. Eventually the dog on the island will get his courage up and swim to shore having overcome his fear of water himself without human force. "Don't force them," the Genthners insist. "If you put the fear of water in them it's hard to get it out."

Young dogs are submissive to older dogs and some of them are ruined as retrievers because they are kenneled or exercised together. A young dog that gets pummeled by a bigger dog every time he tries to do anything is apt to develop a "let George do it" attitude that can affect his trainability later. Pups that get snapped at or have retrieved objects stolen away from them by bigger dogs get nervous about retrieving and may drop the idea out of fear that it will always lead to trouble.

"A lot of retrievers today are a little soft," Paul Genthner notes.

Enthusiastic water work is the result of careful introduction to water when the dog was a pup. Some excellent water retrievers are born without a natural liking for water and can be made fearful of water by early force or a frightening experience.

"They lack the desire and boldness that is going to make them retrievers no matter what. But these same dogs can often be trained to become perfectly adequate gundogs if care is taken to avoid scaring them off early in their lives. In many cases these softer dogs are easier for the average hunter to handle once they have been trained. Starting them right is the key to how well they can be trained later."

(7)

Introduction To Gunfire

Gunshyness is the easiest problem to cause and the hardest to cure of all gundog faults. Luckily it is also easy to prevent gunshyness from developing. There is no reason why your dog should ever become gunshy, for gunshyness is almost always a manmade fault.

You'd be surprised how many dog owners still harbor the old mistaken belief that they should shoot over a new dog "to see if he's gunshy." Don't do it! Shooting over a new pup or older dog is the surest way to *make* a dog fear the sound of a gun. Nevertheless, there are still dog owners who shoot next to a new dog's kennel or even go so far as to take the new dog to a gun club and tie him within sight of a line of shooters, thinking they are going to get the dog accustomed to gunfire. Instead, the dog may be terrified by the experience and can become incurably gunshy because it's owner failed to introduce the gun by more gradual means. Once a dog has been made gunshy there is no sure way to cure him, and even the most patient and lengthy attempts to overcome his fear will probably fail. Once a dog has been made gunshy he's worthless and the chances that he can be cured are, at best, very, very slim.

Learn to prevent gunshyness. Here's how.

Don't Rush the Gun

No matter whether you are raising a litter of puppies, have just bought a pup or older dog, the precautions you must take are the same. Don't be in a rush to expose the dog to gunfire. Take it slow and easy.

Begin by getting the pup accustomed to loud noises. When you're mixing the dog's dinner make an extra amount of noise. Clang the food dish, slam the door, rattle the food bin. Go out of your way to make feeding time noisier than it has to be. The dog will quickly learn to connect those noises with the pleasurable knowledge that dinner is coming, and any nervousness that the loud noises may cause will be overcome.

In litters of young pups there is great peer influence. The pups bolster each other's confidence. If one pup has a tendency to be a little nervous about loud noises, the fact that his brothers and sisters don't share his fear will build his confidence. The shy pup will become more able to accept loud noise when he sees that the rest of his litter is unaffected by it.

The noises you make while preparing dinner become signals that food is on it's way and any fear of noise will be further overcome as a shy pup acquaints your clangs and bangs with the pleasure of eating. Dinner time is totally absorbing to a dog. When your dog has his face in his plate, nothing else will keep his attention for long. It's the perfect time to introduce the sound of the gun.

After acquainting your dog with your noisy dinner-making routine, he should have reached a stage where no amount of noise you make will have any adverse affect. Don't introduce the gun until this stage is reached.

Once you determine that the time is right, mix dinner with your usual clatter and load a single .22 blank cartridge in a gun. Set the dinner down with a bang, slam the kennel gate and walk off about a hundred feet and fire one shot. Chances are the pup will stop eating and stare in your direction. The dog may jump at the shot. He may even back away from his dish. Don't shoot again. One shot with a .22 at a hundred feet is enough for the first time. By the time you have holstered your gun the dog will have forgotten the sound and will be giving his dinner his full attention again.

If the dog shows an unusual amount of concern after hearing the shot, don't make a fuss about it. Don't run up and try to soothe his fears. If you do that he's likely to think the shot scared you, too, and may attach more importance to it. After the shot ignore the pup no matter how he reacts. Show him that the shot did not scare you by simply continuing about your business. Let his dinner do the soothing.

For a week follow that routine. Mix a noise dinner, march off a hundred feet and fire a single shot. By the end of the week the dog will hardly miss a bite when it hears the gun go off. During the second week fire a couple of shots while the dog is eating. After that you can shoot several times, but keep the distance at a hundred feet, don't use a gun heavier than a .22 and only shoot while the dog is eating.

Once a pup or older dog has demonstrated over several weeks that a shot fired while he is eating causes no fear, you can begin to reduce the distance. Fire one at 75 feet. If that causes no fear, next evening fire a shot at 50 feet. Gradually shorten the distance until you can set the dog's dinner down in front of him and fire a shot into the air

Don't take your dog hunting until you have carefully introduced it to the sound of the gun. Start by shooting at a distance at feeding time, then gradually shorten the distance. Make the sound of a gun a signal that always preceeds something the dog likes.

from only a few feet away while he is eating. You can now shoot before feeding him, making the shot a signal that it's dinner time and thus making your dog associate gunfire with a pleasurable anticipation.

There is no reason to shoot anything heavier than a .22 around a pup that is less than six months old.

Introducing the Gun in the Field

Introduction of gunfire in the field should be gradual, too. Wait until your pup is more than six months old and is making simple retrieves with great enthusiasm and has shown no fear when shots are fired over him at mealtime. Don't shoot over retrieves until he just loves retrieving and really flies out after a thrown dummy. Once he reaches that degree of fervor, it's safe to shoot a single .22 blank as he runs out for a thrown dummy. Only shoot once and time it so that you shoot when he is about halfway to the dummy and running at top speed. His attention will be so absorbed by getting the dummy that a pup that's been carefully introduced to gunfire while eating, will never miss a step. Keep the caliber light, but now you can begin shooting a few times during every retrieving session. If the dog shows the slightest apprehension, discontinue shooting during retrieves but continue shooting at mealtimes until his confidence is rebuilt. Then try again.

When your dog shows no hesitation when the gun is fired as he goes out to make a retrieve, you can begin using a louder gun. Shoot a light gauge shotgun now as he goes out, but keep the muzzle pointed up and don't shoot until he is halfway to the dummy. Gradually shorten the distance until you can shoot from only a few feet away from him and then throw the dummy.

Before the dog is taken on it's first hunting trip he should have been fuly exposed to shotgun fire at close range and should be totally unaffected by it. Don't take a dog into a blind and shoot a salvo of 12 gauge guns over it until the dog has been exposed to gunfire at graduated distances in this manner and has proven his acceptance of gunfire without any show of timidness.

A dog raised to understand that the sound of a gun means pleasure will grow up to feel the same thrill you do when the guns are brought out and it's time to go hunting.

[40]

(8)

Discipline As A Way Of Life

"A dog is just as happy when he is minding you as he is when he's raising hell; maybe even happier," so said Ed Minoggie of Sauvie Island, Portland Oregon, one of the West Coast's top retriever trainers.

The biggest problems some people have with retrievers stem from developing wrong relationships with their dogs.

Some people seem to live their lives for the amusement of their dogs. They let the dog be the boss. "They're just too lenient," Minoggie said.

"A gundog is your pal, your companion, but he's also supposed to be your servant to the extent that he does what you tell him to do, the way you want him to do it. One of you is going to be the boss and, since you're paying the bills, you better get that job nailed down for yourself," Ed says.

Ed Minoggie raises and trains retrievers within a pattern of obedience that encompasses the dog's entire relationship with his master. Content with the reward of sincere affection they receive for being obedient, the dogs are happy and eager, yet always under control. Ed develops this relationship by insisting upon obedience and clearly showing the dogs how they are to behave.

Take riding in the car for an example. Ed says, "why carry the dog in a crate. He's not learning anything while he's crated. He's just locked up." Instead, Ed advises teaching the dog to ride on the floor of the car. "Show him that's his place and then make him stay there whenever he's in the car with you. You don't want him leaning out the window or licking your face or putting his paws all over the dashboard, so he must have one place where he can lie that's his place. The floor of the front seat is as good a place as any — you can talk to him there, see what he's doing, but make him stay in that place. Once he learns where his place is and sees that he can't get away with moving around, he'll settle down and be happy to ride like that every time."

It's the same in the house. Ed has places where the dogs are to lie when he tells them to. Knowing their places and happy with the praise they get for staying where they are sent, the dogs are comfortable to have in the house. They know they can't race around scattering rugs, nosing company or grabbing food off the table. Obedience. It's a full-time circumstance. Once a dog realizes that he must be obedient *all* the time, not just when you get mad at him, he'll be content to accept a subservient role.

When it comes to field training, a dog that is accustomed to minding is more attentive to his lessons. All gundog problems stem from disobedience; the retriever that breaks when you stand up to shoot has learned that there is a moment when your mind is on your shooting rather than on his behavior. The dog that hunts on his own, disregarding your whistle, is showing you he doesn't think you can do a thing about it. In either case it is up to you to prove that obedience is essential and that you demand it in every case. Only by showing him who's boss and then proving that you can enforce the commands you give can you retain control over the dog.

"Dogs will test you whenever they think they can get away with something," says Ed Minoggie. "You've got to anticipate those tests and be ready to prove you are still the boss. That's easier to accomplish if the dog is accustomed to having obedience demanded of him all the time, at home, in the car, as well as in the field."

Dogs are quite single-minded about obedience training. You can make them perfectly reliable in the training yard, then see them act like they have no idea what you mean when you give them the same command in a different location or under different circumstances.

Dogs that are raised in an aura of obedience are more responsive when it's time for field training. Ed Minoggie believes dogs are happiest and most confident when they understand their behavior boundaries and know how to do what is right.

[43]

For this reason most professional trainers believe that a lesson must be taught in four or more locations before a dog can really be counted on to respond correctly. For instance, if you have taught your dog to sit when you tell him to do so in the yard and have taught him to sit in a certain spot in the house, another spot in the car and a fourth one, say, in a different place outside, you can expect that he will sit wherever you give him the command thereafter. No matter what you are training him to do, the dog will understand the meaning of the command better and be more reliable about responding to it if you move your lessons around from place to place, repeating each lesson in at least four different locations and showing him that you are always willing and able to enforce the commands you give.

A dog that has been raised in an aura of obedience is far more responsive to field training lessons. Because he accepts your authority, he devotes his mind to whatever it is you are teaching. The dog doesn't feel the need to keep testing your limits, having already discovered that you won't accept disobedience.

"Dogs are quick to form habits," Minoggie explains. "If you get your dog in the habit of being obedient, you're way ahead."

In order to prohibit bad habits from getting started, Minoggie discourages all retrieving except when under discipline. Don't let children throw things for retrievers, for instance, unless you are right there to make sure that crisp, snappy responses to commands are demanded. A dog that is permitted to ignore his schooling some of the time is looking for chances to ignore more of it.

Minoggie tends to delay retrieving work until a dog has matured enough to respond to obedience training. "Pups become bored easily," he warns. "You have to guard against training too early and overdoing it. A dog should be eager and happy when he's being trained, not bored or reluctant." Minoggie likes to delay retrieving work until the dog is old enough to eagerly look forward to making retrieves. Then retrieving becomes part of the dog's reward for responding well to the rest of his training.

In Minoggie's view the dog-man relationship should be one founded upon mutual love and respect. You've a responsibility to make sure your dog knows he can expect the reward of real affection when he does your bidding. And he'll respect you once he's found that you are always willing to enforce your commands whenever he tests you.

(9)

The Importance of Fun Dummies

Never forget that all work and no play makes for a very dull retriever. You don't want your dog to drag through its training exercises with its head and tail down and a "not this again" expression on its face. Training should be fun, it should be the activity your dog looks forward to most, excepting only hunting itself. After all, retrieving is your dog's main purpose in life, the dog's duty, to be sure, but retrieving is your dog's greatest reward as well.

The way to keep your dog's spirit up, keep its tail wagging and an attentive look on its face, is to throw plenty of "fun dummies." At random moments during training sessions, let down the bars, forget the rules, and throw a few of dummies just for the hell of it.

Proceed fun time with a cue that you use each time so that the dog knows when school is out. You can suddenly yell, "Hey, hey, hey. . ." or "Okay, okay. . ." and then start winging dummies and letting the dog break, chase and retrieve without any rules.

Your dog will understand the difference and will look forwad to those fun breaks. After a few minutes of such play you'll see the dog's whole attitude become more relaxed and happy. Now you can bring the dog back into line with a firm "sit" and proceed with training.

(10)

Basic Training

Before your dog can be trained as a retriever it must first be schooled to respond reliably to four commands; come, sit, no, and heel. Obedience to these commands are what make the difference between a canine hunting companion and a hoodlum.

Teaching a pup to come when it is called can begin at infant age, and a good young start to this training puts the pup in a receptive frame of mind in which you start right off being the boss.

Most any little puppy will come if you get down on one knee, call it's name, clap your hands, and say firmly "come." When the pup comes romping up, praise and pat him happily repeating "come, come." From time to time it's a good idea to reward the pup with a morsel of food, but for the most part, your praise should be reward enough.

As the pup gets larger, use the "come" command in circumstances when you know the pup is going to come anyway. When it's outside and you are ready to let the pup come in, call its name and say "come." At feeding time call his name and say "come," and set the food pan down when it responds. By using the come command when

The checkcord is used to convince a pup that it must run directly to you when told to come. Say the pup's name, then the command COME, and pull him to you fast.

the pup is going to come anyway, you start the habit of having the pup come when it's called.

You will also benefit by not using the come command at times when the pup is likely to ignore you. Don't give a command you are not in a position to enforce.

As the pup develops and gains confidence it will also begin to test you. When it reaches the stage where it refuses to come when called or runs off playfully when you call, it's time to start using a collar and a length of line and to begin asserting yourself as boss. You needn't be rough or angry. Simply attach a line to the pup's collar, call its name and say "come" and firmly pull the pup to you and praise it for coming. Do this several times. The pup will understand that you are in control and will not resist for long if you reward it with praise every time it responds properly and put a line on it and pull it to you whenever it refuses.

[48]

The Come In Whistle

Once your pup is reliable at coming when called it's time to teach it that two short beeps on your whistle also means come. Next time you call the pup's name and tell it to *come*, follow the command with two short whistle blasts. From now on, whenever you tell the pup to *come* you will combine the verbal command with the whistle signal.

Next start giving the whistle signal first and the verbal command right after it. Now the pup will begin to respond to the whistle in anticipation of the verbal command. Once your pup understands that the two short whistle blasts and the verbal command mean the same thing, you can drop the verbal command and use it only as a reminder when the pup is slow at responding to the whistle. For the rest of its life the dog will hear the whistle alone sometimes and the verbal command at others and should be quick in responding to either.

A dog that is pokey about coming when called can be speeded up by running away after giving the COME command. He'll come to catch up with you. Then praise him.

Older dogs that have been thoroughly schooled in the meaning of the verbal and whistle commands to *come* can be made even more quick in their response when the variable intensity electronic collar is used. Set at the lowest intensity to which the dog responds, the trainer presses the button and gives the dog low-level electric stimulation at the same moment the *come* whistle is blown. The button is held down until the dog turns and begins to come in, at which moment electric stimulation is stopped. The dog learns it can turn off the unpleasant sensation by responding to the command. Once it learns that it can avoid electric stimulation altogether by responding instantly, the dog will become very quick in responding correctly and will react happily because it knows how to avoid unpleasantness.

The Sit Command

It's best not to try to train the pup to sit at the same time it's learning to come when called. Get the *come* command firmly established first. Once that is accomplished the *sit* command should be taught.

Have the pup walk at your side on a leash. Stop walking and pull up on the leash and collar as you say "sit," simultaneously using your free hand to press the pup's hindquarters to the ground. Pat the pup's chest and repeat the command "sit, sit" as you hold it in place with the leash. Some trainers begin by holding a tidbit over the pup's head and moving it backward over the pup as they hold it in place with the leash and say "sit." The pup's effort to watch the tidbit going back over its head will cause it to sit and it is given the tidbit as a reward.

With repetition the pup will learn the meaning of the command and will sit whenever you tell it to and pull upwards on the leash. It will no longer need to have its rear end pressed down. You can use a light training stick to tap the pup on the stern as a reminder when you give the command.

As the pup's proficiency progresses, walk with it on the leash, stopping from time to time and making it sit on command. Then drop the leash and walk away, repeating the *sit* command and when the pup rises to come after you, grab the leash, pull the pup back into place and make it sit. Keep doing this until you can make the pup sit on command and walk around it and away from it without it rising.

The Whistle Sit

Now that the dog fully understands the *sit* command and will obey it reliably, it's time to teach it that a single blast on your training whistle means the same thing. With the dog leashed at your side give the *sit* command and follow it with a single whistle blast. Several times give the command and whistle signal together, demanding a proper response each time. Once the dog is responding well, drop the verbal command give the whistle signal alone. If the dog does not respond, pull up on the leash and press its haunches down, and repeat the whistle signal. With repetition you will have a dog that sits on either the verbal command or the whistle signal.

At that point begin increasing the distance between you and the dog. When it is running a few yards away dragging a checkcord, blow the whistle signal. If the dog fails to sit instantly, use the checkcord to pull it back to where it was when you whistled and repeat the signal, forcing the dog to sit if necessary. Repetition and gradually increasing the distance will result in a dog that can be stopped at any distance and made to sit when one blast of the whistle is given.

Variable intensity electronic collars are useful in this training once the dog demonstrates that it fully understands the meaning of the command and whistle signal by reliable obedience. Set at the lowest level of intensity to which the dog responds, the collar can be strapped around the dog's loins so that the receiver is on top of its back. When the sit command is given the trainer simultaneously presses the button and holds it down until the dog sits. It will sit to get away from the sensation on its back. When it sits the electronic stimulation is stopped. The dog learns that it can shut off the stimulation by sitting on command. As it speeds up its response in order to shut off the stimulation sooner the trainer can eliminate the stimulation and let the dog see that a quick response to the command avoids the unpleasant sensation. This method will lead to a very crisp response to the command at any distance. When the dog slows its response, the trainer uses the electronic stimulation again.

Teaching to Heel

Retrievers should be taught to heel on the side on which you do not normally carry your gun when hunting. Right or left makes no

A dog at heel should be trained to keep its head even with its handler's knee. The dog should walk on the opposite side from that on which the handler carries a shotgun.

difference, you heel the dog on whichever side is your safest side.

You'll need a light training stick, leash and collar and later, a pocket full of gravel.

Repeating the command "heel" you walk forward with the dog held in position on your safe side. If it forges ahead, rap it lightly across the front knees with the training stick. If it drags behind, pull it forward with the leash and reach around behind yourself with the training stick to rap its hind legs.

At first you will perform this exercise walking straight ahead. Once the dog gets the idea and begins to stay in position when you tell it to heel, start making right angle turns to the right and left and use the leash and stick to keep the dog in position while you make the turns. Whenever the dog gets out of position order it to "heel" in a firm voice and use the stick and leash to bring it back into position.

Dogs quickly pick up the meaning of this command and become pretty good heelers in a few sessions. But there's a wide spread between pretty good and the college level heeling you see from fully trained dogs. To get the dog to heel perfectly involves making heeling more challenging to the dog. Your dog will respond to the challenge if you create situations in which the dog has to keep attentive to what you're going to do next. Once the dog is good at remaining in the proper heel position while you make right and left and right angle turns, then begin stopping, telling the dog to *sit* and then taking a step backwards and ordering it to *heel*. You'll have to pull the dog backwards into position the first few times and you will have to hold the dog away from you as you pull it back to keep it from trying to turn towards you and bumping against your legs. Keep practicing until the dog will step backwards into the heeling position. Then tell it to sit and give praise and pats. Your aim is to bring the dog along to the point where it will leap backwards into the *heel* position on command. Working beside a fence helps by limiting the dog's escape options.

At each step in the dog's development you keep it on a leash until it is capable of staying at heel without requiring pressure from the leash or reminders from the training stick. When that point is reached, it's time to take the leash off and try the same maneuvers without any form of restraint. The dog will recognize this freedom and may test your ability to enforce your command now that the leash is gone. Now is the time to have your pocket full of small gravel.

In advanced heeling training the dog should keep even with your knee as you walk in right angle patterns in both forward and backward directions.

When the dog forges ahead order it to *heel*. If it fails to respond immediately, fling the gravel at it. Whether you actually hit the dog with some of the gravel or just have a near miss probably won't matter. The dog will be so surprised by the sound of the stuff rattling down around him that it will streak back into the heel position with a look of wonder on its face. It didn't know you could reach out like that.

Heeling on Line

With the dog sitting beside you, turn your position to face the four points of the compass, ordering the dog to adjust its position to match yours. At this stage you should position the knee closest to the dog ahead when you turn towards the dog and slightly behind when you turn away from it. In attempting to keep its head even with your knee when ordered to heel, the dog will tend to turn with you more readily if you position your knee in this manner.

All the rest is just practice.

The No Command

You can't communicate with dogs in sentences. It may make you feel good to say, "Get out of the garbage!" or "Keep your damn paws off my shirt!", but it will be alot easier for the dog to comprehend that it is doing something wrong if you limit your expletives to one word, "NO!" It should be said harshly and loudly whenever the dog is doing something you don't want done and it's meaning to the dog should be "Stop whatever you are doing NOW!" Until the dog is fully cognizant of this meaning the command should be backed up with physical force to make positive that the negative behavior is eliminated immediately.

Once your dog comprehends the meaning of the *No* command and reacts to it and the menacing sound of your voice, less physical force will be needed. But the dog should never forget that No will be enforced if it doesn't stop whatever it is doing.

It is a good idea to follow the *No* command with a positive command so that the dog understands how it can do something right to rectify the situation. Once your dog is responding well to the *No* command, begin following it with another command. Shout "NO!" and when the dog stops whatever it's doing, tell it to *come* or *sit* or *heel*. Later, when you are teaching the dog to take hand signals, this foundation will be helpful. You'll be able to stop the dog with a "NO!" and then give it an *"Over"* or a *"Back."*

Come, sit, no and heel; four words that makes the difference between a gentleman and a bum.

(11)

Honoring

At all stages of training it will help to work with other trainers and their dogs whenever possible. If you have a friend with a retriever, train together often. If you haven't a friend with a retriever, find one. This may best be done by joining a hunting retriever club. You can find out where there is one near you by writing to the addresses listed in Chapter One.

Training a retriever is a job that is easier to accomplish when two people are involved. You need one person to work the dog and another to throw birds and dummies and shoot in a lot of training situations.

You also want to teach your dog to honor, that is to sit and wait patiently when another dog is sent to retrieve. Teaching dogs to honor is more than just good manners. The dog that grows up understanding that it does not get sent to make every retrieve becomes more obedient and therefore more willing to remain under control when you do send it.

Whenever possible, throughout the training process, alternate with another trainer and his dog. Have one dog sit and watch while the other dog is worked. Use the sit command, a leash, and a rap across the rump with the training stick to enforce honoring.

Working dogs in groups helps each dog learn that it must wait to be sent and that only dogs that are steady get retrieves. Dogs that know that they don't get a retrieve every time something falls learn to wait their turn and become more obedient.

Watching another dog work will heighten your dog's keenness to go out fast when his turn comes, and getting accustomed to waiting for his turn will make him a calmer more manageable dog in every other respect.

(12)

Hard Mouth — Easier Prevented Than Cured

"Hard mouth," the tenacious desire some dogs have to crush and chew birds which they have been sent to retrieve, is a fault that has rendered worthless many an otherwise decent retriever. It's a fault that crops up in all retrieving breeds and once hard mouth has become a habit, it is one of the most difficult faults to correct.

At times the cause is hereditary, but more often than not, dogs develop hard mouths because of oversights on the parts of their trainers. In most cases hard mouth could have been prevented if the trainer had used some common sense and followed a few simple rules during the dog's critical early formative stages.

The renowned professional retriever trainer Joe Riser of Rutledge, Georgia, shares every retriever trainer's abiding anxiety over dogs that occasionally decide to eat a bird they have been sent to retrieve. Consequently, Joe Riser has studied carefully how hard mouth can be prevented.

Here's how he does it:

From the day a pup comes under his observation Joe Riser watches for early signs of hard mouth. A dog that tends to mouth dummies roughly and is reluctant to release a bird or dummy it has

[59]

retrieved has commonplace faults and can usually be made into a gentle-mouthed retriever, given experience and careful training. The problem cases are those dogs that absolutely rip apart and destroy retrieving objects. Dogs in this second category are sometimes incurable and may at best become dogs that are reliable only when the threat of punishment is near at hand.

Often hard mouth tendencies are started simply by someone giving young dogs hard objects to play with or retrieve. "Always start young dogs with soft canvas dummies, not sticks or even plastic dummies," Joe warns. "If a dog is chomping down on a canvas dummy you can see his teeth marks and reprimand him. But a dog that is given a hard object to retrieve may be bearing down with great jaw strength and never leave a sign that tips you off to the fact that trouble is developing."

To make it easy for a young dog to pick up and cary a dummy without having to bite down hard, Joe uses small-size dummies. These are made of canvas and filled with excelsior or sawdust and are only about two inches in diamter.

From the time a dog is four months to a year old, he goes through several teething stages which will make him want to chew things. During this phase it's a good idea to give him some definite chewing toys — a rawhide bone, perhaps. But don't ever let him chew his retrieving dummies. When his teething stages are at their worst you may have to hold off on retrieving games for a while. He's too young for firm discipline and you don't want to impair his retrieving instinct by cracking down on him too hard for doing something which seems perfectly natural.

The way you take a dummy away from a dog once it has been retrieved is important. Joe Riser presses down on the dummy so that the pressure is against the dog's lower jaw, then he twists the dummy as he takes it from the dog's mouth. The action is quick and decisive and it does much to prevent tug of war games from getting started. If the dog is one that does clamp down on a dummy and refuse to let go, Joe rolls the dog's upper lip under a canine tooth and presses hard saying "leave it!" until the dog drops the dummy in his hand.

These methods work if employed when hard mouth tendencies are just beginning to be formed. Later, if hard mouth has been allowed to become a habit, much firmer methods must be used and even they are only about 50% successful.

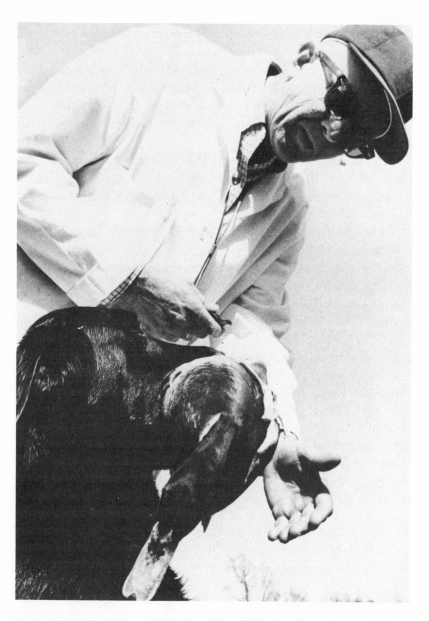

Preventing hard mouth means heading off trouble before it begins. Joe Riser works dogs on shackled live ducks in training sessions before permitting them to retrieve live cripples.

Often a pup that has been trained carefully with dummies shows his first inclination to become hard-mouthed when feathered game is introduced. To the best of your knowledge he's never chomped down on a dummy but he wants to flatten every pigeon or duck you throw for him. Again, the preventive method is easier than the cure.

Joe Riser introduces young retrievers to feathers early in the game by tying first a few quill feathers, later a clean bird wing to the retrieving dummy the pup is accustomed to. If the pup shows any desire to clamp down or chew, Joe pinches the dog's lip against his teeth and orders him to "leave it."

Early introduction to feathers in this way lessens the drama of the moment when the dog gets his first taste of feathered game and reduces the excitement that may cause a dog to bite down when he first gets a bird in his mouth.

When the pup is fully accustomed to retrieving dummies with feathers attached, and delivering gently, Joe introduces a freshly killed frozen pigeon. Holding the pigeon in his hand he teases the dog with it until the dog reaches to take the bird. Then Joe places the bird in the dog's mouth and gently closes its jaws over the bird saying, "fetch, fetch." With his hand under the dog's jaw to prevent him from spitting the bird out, Joe encourages the dog to hold the bird for up to a minute, then he commands "leave it," and pinches the dog's lip over his teeth if it fails to drop the bird into Joe's hand immediately.

From such an introduction it follows that you work into short retrieves using the fresh-killed frozen pigeon. After each retrieve Joe examines the bird carefully to check for damage. Should he find signs that the dog has bitten down hard he goes back a step, having the dog hold the bird for long periods and pinching the dog's lip over his teeth at the first sign of clamping down.

Joe feels that a freshly killed frozen pigeon is preferable to an unfrozen bird since it is firmer and easier for the dog to grasp. Also it's important to de-emphasize the meat aspect when dead game is first introduced. A soft, warm, bloody bird may remind the dog of dinner and the results may be disastrous.

Another critical time when retrievers may show their first inclination to be hard mouthed occurs when the dog first meets crippled game. Since his role will be most important when a crippled bird is down and lost, you want your retriever to be fully schooled

When taking delivery from your retriever take the bird with a downward motion and avoid pulling the bird away from the dog in a manner which would encourage a tug of war response.

in bringing back cripples without damaging them further.

Once the dog is large enough to carry a duck and has been successfully retrieving frozen and fresh dead pigeons, Joe brings out the shackled mallard.

"One of the biggest mistakes a retriever owner can make is to take a dog hunting before he has been thoroughly schooled in retrieving shackled game," Joe warns. "Chances are he'll either turn out cripply-shy because he runs into a sassy old bird that pecks him, or he'll kill the cripple out of self-defense and begin a habit that will prove very hard to correct."

Depending on the type of game you hunt you'll want to use either mallards shackled with their wings tied together over their backs with soft cloth tapes, or pheasants shackled with their feet tied together and their wing feathers clipped short.

Introduction is the same as with the frozen pigeon; you place the shackled bird in the dog's mouth and command him to "fetch," holding your hand beneath his jaw to prevent him from spitting it out. On the command "leave it," he should drop the bird in your hand. If he hangs on, roll his lip over his tooth and bear down hard repeating "leave it," until he releases.

Once successful in getting the dog to hold the live shackled bird for a minute or so, begin with short retrieves. After each retrieve examine the bird for damage, never permitting the dog to start clamping down on the bird. Gradually, work up to longer retrieves, water retrieves and finally blind retrieves.

Dogs that are trained from puppyhood according to these precautionary methods rarely decide to damage the dead or crippled game they are called on to retrieve during actual hunting situations. The method works because it heads off trouble before it begins; the puppy is not given hard chewable objects to retrieve, it has other chewing toys during his teething stages. It gets used to feathers being attached to his retrieving dummies before encountering feathered game. The game it first encounters is fresh and frozen, easy to retrieve without messing it up. The dog learns how to handle live shackled game before meeting it's first cripple.

(13)

Force Training Retrievers

There was a time when force training most retrievers to retrieve was unnecessary; their natural instincts were so strong that refusal to retrieve was unheard of. Well, times have changed. The enormous pet market for retrievers has fostered a great deal of indescriminate breeding and an unfortunate result is that the retriever gene pool has been diluted to the extent that many registered retrievers born today have weakened retrieving instincts. These days most professional trainers force break their prospects to retrieve regardless of how much or how little natural retrieving instinct the dogs retain.

"A natural retriever retrieves for himself, a force broke retriever retrieves for you," says Omar Driskill professional retriever trainer who operates Choctaw Kennels in Simsboro, La.

Force breaking takes time, patience and repetition, but the result is a dog that retrieves eagerly every time it is sent. Force breaking makes retrieving something the dog does as a result of training rather than a game it plays when it feels like it. Once the training is complete, force-broken retrievers become happy and eager in their work because they feel rewarded for successfully responding to commands. In this atmosphere the dog's retrieves become faster and more precise as the dog learns how to succeed.

Force breaking can be done at any age after a pup has grown its adult teeth, and is most commonly applied when dogs have reached about a year of age and have been taught to come, sit and heel.

There are several methods of force training retrievers, all of which rely on causing the dog to open its mouth in response to slight pain which is removed instantly when it takes a retrieving dummy into its mouth and holds it. The dog quickly learns that it can stop the pain by reaching out to grab the dummy when ordered to "fetch" and holding it until told to "drop." Eventually, the dog learns it can avoid the pain altogether by grabbing the dummy instantly when ordered to "fetch." Then it's just a matter of increasing the distances gradually. The result is a dog that fully understands the meaning of the word "fetch" and knows that it can avoid unpleasantness by responding to the command instantly.

The most commonly used method for force breaking retrievers depends on the ear pinch to make the dog open it's mouth on command. "I like the ear pinch better than the toe-pinch or nerve-hitch because the ear is handier," says Omar Driskill. "It's easier to grab a dog by the collar and fold it's ear back over the buckle than it is to get hold of it's foot."

For this the dog should wear a wide collar which has a heavy roller-type buckle with a thick protruding stud. When the time comes, you will pinch the ear by grasping the dog's collar with your fingers under the strap and folding the dog's ear back over the stud on the buckle with your thumb. Increased thumb pressure will cause the dog to open it's mouth when you command "fetch."

Choose a special place to carry out the force training lessons. You should work in the shade and away from distractions. You'll need a sturdy table that will support the weight of the dog without wobbling.

At first you'll work with the dog on the table. Being up off the ground takes the dog out of its own element and puts it entirely within your control. There should be an overhead limb, beam or cable to which you can attach a line from the dog's collar in order to prevent the dog from leaping off the table. Plan to work with two lightweight training dummies, one for the actual lessons and a second which you stuff in your back pocket to have ready for instant use if the dog inadvertently drops the first out of your reach.

Force retriever training begins with the dog on a table, tied overhead so that it cannot jump off. Shouting is never necessary, the ear pinch is the only force used. The process takes three solid weeks of daily work.

Rolling the dog's ear back over the stud on its collar, pinch the ear against the stud until the dog opens its mouth to complain. Then pop the dummy into its mouth and gently close its jaws, saying FETCH and supporting the dog's chin so it cannot spit the dummy out.

Put the dog on the table and attach the line from his collar to the overhead beam. Pat the dog and reassure it. Get it accustomed to being up on the table before proceeding with the first lesson. When the dog is at ease you are ready to begin. Make each lesson last about ten minutes and try to hold several sessions each day until the dog responds eagerly and reliably every time.

Stage One: No ear pinch. Gently open the dog's mouth and place the dummy in its mouth taking care to avoid pinching its lips. Close the dog's jaws on the dummy and say the word "hold." Tap the dog's lower jaw with your fingers to keep it's mouth shut on the dummy and repeat, "hold, hold." After a few seconds say "drop," and let the dog drop the dummy into your hand. Give lavish praise and then repeat.

The dog should be proficient at holding the dummy you place in its mouth until you tell it to drop before you proceed. Several ten minute sessions may be needed to get the dog to hold the dummy.

Stage Two: With the dog on the table, repeat the holding exercise

When you first go from the table to the ground you will have to begin at the beginning again. Pinch the dog's ear against its collar stud and order it to FETCH as you push its head down towards the dummy.

and give praise when the dog does it right. This puts the dog in a relaxed mood. Now grasp its collar with your fingers under the strap, fold the ear back over the buckle with your thumb and command "fetch" in a firm tone, simultaneously increasing pressure with your thumb and repeating "fetch" until the dog opens its mouth to yelp when the pressure becomes intolerable. When the dog opens his mouth instantly pop the dummy into its mouth saying "hold," and relieve the pressure on the ear. Use your fingers to tap the dog under the chin to make him keep holding until you say "drop." Praise the dog, then repeat. Each time pinch the ear until the dog opens its mouth, then pop the dummy in and have the dog hold the dummy for several seconds before telling it to *drop*.

After several experiences the dog will learn to anticipate the ear pinch and will begin to open its mouth to take the dummy as soon as you give the "fetch" command. That's progress. Now make it start reaching for the dummy by holding the dummy several inches out in front of it. Always hold the ear folded over the buckle so that you can pinch it if necessary, but don't pinch when the dog obeys instantly. Let it learn that it can avoid the ear pinch by obeying, but be ready to apply the pinch the instant the dog gets sloppy. If the dog refuses to drop the dummy on command, pinch the ear to force it to open its mouth and obey.

Once the dog will reach out to grab the dummy on command, start lowering the dummy so that the dog has to reach down to grab it. You may have to reapply the ear pinch when the dummy is offered at this new position. When the dog will reach out, down and up to take the dummy, place the dummy on the table at the dog's feet and force it to pick the dummy up off the table and hold it. As the dog becomes more proficient, make it hold the dummy for several seconds before telling it to *drop*. While it is holding the dummy, tap the dummy with your fingers so that the dog will firm up its grip. Don't let it drop the dummy until you tell it to.

Stage Three: Now you have the dog reaching to grab the dummy when ordered to *fetch* and picking it up off the table and holding it until told to *drop*. Next you take the dog off the table and place it on the ground. Attach a short lead to the dog's collar and make it repeat it's earlier lessons. You may find that the dog needs its ear pinched several times before it comprehends that the commands it learned on the table must also be followed on the ground. Once the

Next begin lengthening the distance but keep a checkcord on the dog in order to prevent wandering and speed up the retrieves. If the dog balks, force it with another ear pinch and shorten the distance until the dog does it right.

dog is again reaching to grab the dummy on command, start making it take a few steps walking at heel carrying the dummy before you tell it to drop. Keep at this until you can toss the dummy on the ground and have the dog pick it up and carry it as you walk through various heeling maneuvers. Keep repeating this lesson several times each day for at least a week until the dog is not only proficient at following the commands, but happy in its knowledge that it is responding correctly. Remember to praise the dog in a happy tone of voice when it is doing well. Never lose your temper, just continue patiently repeating the lesson until the dog gets it right every time.

Stage Four: Now it's time to begin throwing the dummy a short distance from the dog and sending it for short retrieves. For this attach a 30-foot checkcord to the dog's collar so that you can pull the dog back briskly to you when it has picked up the thrown dummy. If the dog refuses a retrieve at this point, take it by the collar and rush it over to the dummy and use the ear pinch to make it pick the dummy up as you command *"fetch."* Then order it to *"hold"* and rush back to the spot where you were, commanding *"hold,"* and using the ear pinch again to force the dog to pick the dummy up if it drops it before commanded to do so.

When you send the dog for a thrown retrieve say *"fetch"* as you let it go. As the dog picks the dummy up, command *"come"* and pull it straight to you with the checkcord. Do not permit dawdling or playing with the dummy. Use the ear pinch to correct slow pickups or dropping of the dummy. Make the dog sit beside you, then say "drop," and take it from him.

Throughout the training be sure that the dog is always carrying the dummy with a firm grip. It should not toss the dummy in its mouth, drop it or carry it loosely. You can firm up its grip by telling the dog to *"hold"* and tapping the dummy with your fingers. If you can knock it out of the dog's mouth doing this, the dog was holding too loosely and needs to firm its grip.

If that happens, it helps to make the dog retrieve heavier objects. A dummy filled with sand may work. Omar Driskill sometimes tightens up a dog's grip by making it retrieve a chunk of firewood. Weighted dummies are also sold by dog supply houses for this purpose.

The final stage is to replace the dummy with a frozen pigeon-Watch for signs of hard mouth and stop any such tendencies at once.

If the dog has no problem with frozen pigeons, move on to using frozen ducks and, finally, live shackled ducks.

Using the Electronic Collar

Trainers who have electronic collars should not use them in force retrieving until all of the foregoing lessons have been completely mastered by the dog. But once the dog has been fully force trained and is a reliable retriever, a variable intensity electronic collar can be useful in increasing the speed with which the dog completes each retrieve.

The collar should be set at the level to which the dog reacts but does not show fright or pain. The trainer shakes the dummy in front of the dog to get it excited and then says "fetch" at the same instant pressing the button to deliver low-level electronic stimulation. The button is released the instant the dog grabs the dummy. The dog learns that it can turn off the unpleasant stimulation by obeying the command. Progress through the standard steps, having the dog pick the dummy up off the ground and finally running out to get the dummy and bringing it back. Start with very short retrieves and gradually lengthen the distance. At each stage deliver the electronic stimulation as you give the command and stop it as soon as the dog reaches top speed in its effort to get to the dummy. The dog will learn that it can stop the unpleasant sensation by going out fast. When the dog reaches the point where it starts bursting out fast when the command is given, don't shock it at all. Let the dog learn that it can avoid the unpleasant sensation altogether by going out fast. From then on only use the stimulation when the dog falters or dawdles. Used in this manner the variable intensity electronic collar can effectively make dogs run fast all the way out and all the way back on long distance retrieves.

Caution: Before using the electronic collar in force retrieving, the dog should have been trained to come, sit and heel with the electronic collar so that it already understands that it can shut off the stimulation by responding quickly to the command. Don't ever use the shock collar in any retrieving exercise on a dog which has not been collar-trained on simple obedience commands first!

One of the great side benefits of force training dogs to retrieve is that it makes the dog more receptive to all other training lessons and

Keep a spare dummy in your back pocket whenever you're training. You'll be surprised how many times you'll need it.

establishes you as the trainer and the dog as trainee; a very important distinction for the dog to comprehend.

The key to success is daily repetition. Don't skip a day. Commit yourself to at least one ten minute session each day for three weeks and you'll have the job done right. Fetch, come, sit, drop. That's the drill.

(14)

Training Retrievers To Mark Off The Gun

Marking, the ability to note and remember exactly where a bird falls, is one of the most important qualities a good hunting retriever must possess. Good marking ability enables a retriever to find fallen birds without having to be directed to them by its handler and, thereby, reduces the disruption of a hunt. A good marker will remember multiple falls and learns to recognize the difference in the way dead birds and cripples fall from the air. When sent out to fetch and allowed to choose which bird to go after first, a good marker with a lot of hunting experience will even learn to streak out after a cripple first, knowing that birds that fall dead can wait.

Good marking ability depends upon good eyesight, to be sure, but it is a quality which can be developed and expanded by certain training techniques. Any dog's marking ability can be improved immensely by training the way Omar Driskill does it.

Omar Driskill is a duck hunter whose interest in retriever training is entirely devoted to improving retrievers for hunting use. In his professional career he has turned out more than 2,000 trained hunting retrievers and is the founding father of the national Hunting Retriever Club, Inc. The dogs he trains are noted for their outstanding ability to mark and remember where birds fall.

Teaching a dog to mark means teaching him to look where your gun is pointing," says Omar, and with those few words he has revolutionized how retrievers should be trained.

Consider this; according to traditional retriever training methods the handler stands beside the dog and says "Mark" at the moment when a distant bird boy shoots a gun and throws a bird in the air. The sound of the gun attracts the dog's attention and it looks in that direction in time to see the thrown bird falling. That's the way marking has been practiced for years.

Then along comes Omar Driskill, the duck hunter. He noticed immediately that retrievers trained by this method were poor markers when they were confronted with actual hunting situations in which there is no one out there attracting the dogs attention to the place where a bird is going to fall. Seated in a duck blind these dogs didn't know where to look when the men around them suddenly jumped up and started shooting. Often these dogs would watch the birds flying away and miss seeing those that fell. Consequently, they would have to be directed to unseen "blind" falls by their handlers. This meant that the handler would have to get out of the duck blind and stand at the water's edge blowing whistles and waving his arms to give hand signals in order to direct the dog to a fallen bird which could easily have been retrieved without help if the dog had simply known where to look when the shooting was going on.

All this commotion creates an unnecessary interruption of the hunt and, if ducks are flying, some good shooting will be missed out on while the handler works his dog. "Hunting retrievers should mark every bird that falls and do as much retrieving as possible without requiring help from their handlers," Omar concluded.

"There's no bird boy out there attracting the dog's attention to the right spot when you're duck hunting," he points out. "The dog has to know where to look."

Omar Driskill teaches dogs where to look by schooling them to mark off the end of his shotgun barrel. Instead of having the bird boy shoot or yell to attract the dog's attention, Omar does the shooting from the dog's side just as you do when hunting. He uses a shotgun, not a training pistol. With an exaggerated gesture he raises his gun in the direction where the distant bird boy will be

Omar Driskill trains his dogs to mark off the end of the gun barrel. He shoots and a bird boy throws a bird or dummy in the distance where the gun is pointed. Dogs learn to follow the swinging gun barrel to see the distant action.

throwing and touches off a blank cartridge. The shot is the signal for the bird boy to throw a dummy or shackled bird in a high arc where the dog can see it clearly. As the bird falls Omar keeps his shotgun at his shoulder pointing in the direction of the fall. If the dog fails to see the mark he repeats the procedure as many times as is necessary to get the dog looking in the direction of the shot. It will help to start by having your dog watch another dog work this way.

In early lessons if the dog has trouble recognizing that the bird always falls in the direction where Omar's shotgun is pointing, he may have the bird boy give a little extra help by yelling "Bang!" or shooting a blank pistol just before throwing. But the bird boy's efforts always follow the firing of Omar's shotgun from the dog's side.

"Dogs get the hang of this very quickly," Omar explains. "We train this way every day and dogs are very quick to put it together. In almost no time they start turning their heads in the direction I'm pointing my shotgun and they see each bird or dummy fall and can

Hunting retriever training puts the shotgun in the hands of the dog handler, not the bird thrower. Just as in real hunting situations, the gun goes off beside the dog and it must watch for a bird to fall out where the gun is pointed. Here Barbara Genthner shoots and Paul does the throwing for a young yellow Lab.

pick it up as a marked retrieve rather than requiring directional handling."

Before a dog is taken duck hunting he must also become accustomed to having shotguns fired very close to him. No matter how thoroughly the dog has been introduced to the sound of gunfire from a distance, you should not wait until you are actually out hunting to let him hear a shotgun go off at close range.

Omar combines marking training with introduction to close range gunfire. In early lessons he has a helper use the shotgun from a position some yards ahead of where he stands beside the seated dog. The helper suddenly points the shotgun in the direction of the hidden bird boy and fires a popper load or a .22 blank from a rifle and the bird boy immediately throws out the bird or dummy. Omar sends it to retrieve only if the dog has seen and marked the fall.

From the dog's position it can see everything that is happening. It sees the helper mount and point the shotgun and just as it hears the shot, a bird appears and falls in the direction the gun was pointing. As the dog begins to comprehend what is happening it will begin to anticipate the bird and will be looking in the direction the gun is pointing as the bird is thrown. Gradually, the helper with the shotgun moves back closer to the dog's seated position, diminishing the distance between dog and gun until the gun can be fired from directly beside the dog. At that point Omar begins using the shotgun himself from beside the seated dog and the shooting assistant is no longer needed. From then on Omar will shoot from beside the dog every time a mark is to be thrown. When dogs trained to mark by this method are taken hunting, they will be fully accustomed to being shot over with loud shotguns and they will know enough to look in the direction that guns are pointed when shots are fired.

As the dog gets proficient at marking off the end of Omar's gun barrel the lessons are made more difficult. The distance to the mark is gradually increased. Instead of having just one mark you progress to having two or even three. When doubles or triples are thrown, Omar swings his shotgun, points and shoots in the direction of each fall, just as if he were hunting. The dogs learn to follow the gun muzzle and see each fall. With practice they become proficient at remembering multiple falls.

"Don't be in a hurry to help the dog by giving him hand signals," Omar warns. "The most helpful hunting retrievers are those that

Work with a partner whenever possible. Here one man shoots while the other stands ready to correct the dog if it breaks. The dog will be allowed to retrieve only when it remains steady until sent by the handler.

need the least amount of help from their handlers." Consequently, Omar gives his dogs time to hunt and find a bird or dummy by the use of their noses and intelligent searching patterns. He gives directional assistance only if the dog strays away from the area of a known fall.

"Even then you should be careful," he cautions. "The bird may be a cripple that has run off. Never forget that the dog is the one with the nose. Let him use it."

When you are training a hunting retriever keep reminding yourself that you are training your dog for actual hunting and make sure your training methods prepare it for the problems it will encounter in the duck blind.

In traditional field trials marking is made easier by having the shooting done out near the spot where the bird boy is going to throw his bird, so field trial training methods put the gun in the hand of the bird boy instead of the handler. But when you are duck hunting the gun will be in your hands and the shooting will be done right over your dog's head. The dog better be able to handle that and know where to look when the guns go off.

This Golden retriever has been trained to mark off the gun barrel. She turns her head as the gun swings and sees which birds are shot.

(15)

The Retriever
Training Box

Despite all that is written about teaching retrievers to take hand signals, the most effective gundogs are those that mark and remember the exact spot where game falls so that when they are sent to retrieve, no hand signals are required. Good markers are the most efficient retrievers and the most enjoyable to take hunting.

Teaching a dog to mark well depends on having the dog sit where it can get a good view of the action but is out of the way of shooters. The dog must remain still as birds approach, watching but not moving or creating a disturbance.

Omar Driskill, the well known gundog retriever trainer who operates Choctaw Kennels, Simsboro, La., has a simple and very effective system all retriever owners can use to enhance their dogs' opportunities to develop steadiness and exceptional marking ability.

You need a double boat snap and a rectangular piece of plywood with low sides forming a box approximately 20 by 30 inches. Omar attaches an eyebolt in the center of one of the short sides of the box so that a dog lying in the box with one end of the snap attached to its collar and the other end snapped to the eyebolt is held in place and cannot stand up. He installs such a dog box outside one end of

Omar Driskell works young dogs for their first hunting season from a shallow-sided box to which the dog is fastened by a double boat snap. The dog can see and mark falls clearly but the box establishes boundaries from which it cannot move. Dogs worked this way quickly recognize the box as their place and are easier to steady since they know where they should be and have never developed a habit of breaking.

every duck blind he uses regularly and has another mobile model that can be carried along and used whenever he chooses to shoot from a location that does not have a dog box.

"A dog needs to know where his place is," Omar explains. "If you always work a dog from a box, he will quickly accept the box as his place and will get in the box automatically when you take him to your blind."

Omar starts working dogs from the box the first time he takes them hunting and keeps them snapped in place throughout the dog's first hunting season.

"When he's snapped in place the dog can't move," he explains. "All the dog can do is lie still and watch. Because he is out where he can see he doesn't have to squirm around to see the action and the snap prevents him from ever rushing out to retrieve before he's sent. He becomes steady by habit and when the time comes to enforce steadiness you'll find that a dog that has had a season of working out of a box has already lost most of it's inclination to break."

Most people tie unsteady dogs in blinds, but they give them too much loose line which enables the dog to move around and then they try to hide the dog in the blind where it can't be seen by approaching waterfowl. The trouble is that a dog that can't be seen also can't see, so it scrambles about to try to get a better view of the action. This is a distraction that gunners resent and the dog's ability to move when guns start going off encourages a habit of breaking which will be harder to correct later.

"Put him right out where he can see," says Omar. "Then snap him in place without any slack so that he can't do anything but lie still. Give any dog a first shooting season with that restraint and you'll wind up with a good marker that is naturally steady."

I have hunted with Omar on the flooded rice fields of northern Louisiana and watched his dogs working from the training boxes. There was one big Chesapeake named Strider whose manners and bird marking ability could not be improved upon.

Omar had started working with the dog when it was about a year old. On Strider's first day of actual hunting Omar snapped him up short in the dog box that was located right beside Omar's shooting position but just outside the blind. A screen of brush was bent over the dog box to hide the dog's body but the dog had a clear view of the decoys and the whole shooting scene.

When ducks came in Strider could only lie quietly watching. When they swept in over the decoys and the gunners stood up to shoot, the snap prevented the big dog from standing up, too. He watched and saw a duck fall and could do nothing but watch it tumble

When hunting in flooded timber dogs are trained to sit on platforms. This hunter uses a deer hunting tree stand set at water level. The Lab knows that is its place.

and hit the water. Omar let the dog mark the spot and remember it for a moment, then reached out and unsnapped Strider and sent him for the retrieve. When the duck was delivered Omar gave the big pup a pat and then ordered "in your box," and snapped Strider in place again. The scenario was repeated each time ducks were shot, the big pup held in place where he could see the action and mark and remember the falls. And each time the retrieves were completed, he was immediately put back in the box and snapped in place. At the end of that morning's shoot, when twelve ducks had been killed and retrieved, Strider completed the last delivery and then jumped into the box voluntarily and lay down in place, ready for the next episode.

"That's all it took with him," Omar said. "One morning of shooting and the dog has learned his place."

Once you try using the training box you will find that your dog not only accepts it but actually becomes more confident when worked from it. The dog no longer has to think about where it should be or whether it can move. Without those distracting temptations, the dog can concentrate on watching and marking falls. You'll be surprised how much better markers dogs become when they are started in the training box.

The box has other uses, too. Put a similar box in a corner of the room where you spend your evenings and snap your pup in it when he is in the house. He will learn that he has a place and that he cannot move around but can comfortably lie still when he is in it. Young dogs that have been introduced to household living by being snapped short in a training box soon accept that the box is their place, their "safety zone", and can be sent to sit or lie there whenever you want to reduce the confusion in the house.

Dogs understand boundaries. A box has a surface area and sides that define the boundaries within which you are telling the dog to stay. When the dog does not have the opportunity to question those boundaries or see how far they can be stretched, it accepts them and stops jumping around.

One day in January I was out sea shooting eiders with Jan White and Bill Gansky off Cundy's Harbor, Maine. When the shooting was over we helped Bill haul some lobster traps and Whistler, my Chesapeake retriever, was confused about where she was supposed to be. Wherever she sat, she was in someone's way, or was threatened by clanking fishing gear that was being hauled aboard. Moving to get out of the way, she was in the way even more.

Remembering Omar Driskill's training box, I took a flat fish box and put it in a corner of the deck and told Whistler to get in it and stay.

She sat in the box with an expression of absolute relief. Now she knew where she was supposed to be. The boundaries were clear. She could forget about trying to improve her position and just enjoy watching what was happening. From then on, whenever we stopped to haul gear, Whistler would jump in the box voluntarily and sit there smiling.

Duck hunters who shoot in flooded timber usually carry treestands which they attach just above the water level for their dogs to sit on. Dogs used in this kind of shooting have no choice, there is no place to sit except on the platform and they readily accept that as their place and need little coaxing to climb aboard. A short strap and snap to prevent the dog from breaking is all the convincing most dogs need to become steady in such situations. Knowing that they can't break or move frees these dogs to concentrate on marking falls and they soon become dogs that can remember multiple marks and do their jobs without requiring assistance from their handlers.

A training box installed in your duck boat will have the same effect. Wherever it is used, the training box will simplify your training process by removing the temptations that distract inexperienced dogs.

(16)

The First Hunting Season

Once your dog has been taught the basics of obedience and force-broken to retrieve, it is ready to go hunting. Until now it's training has consisted of instruction, praise and correction. In hunting season the dog will discover it's true role and the reason for all the training you've been working on will begin to make sense.

At this point the dog has not been trained to remain steady and it has not yet learned to follow hand signals. This season you will concentrate on making hunting and retrieving fallen game the most wonderful experience your dog can imagine.

Since the dog is not steady it's important to prevent it from breaking when ducks are approaching and the guns are going off. To do this you must restrain the dog by fastening it in a place where it will be able to witness the action and see where the birds fall but not run out to retrieve until you send it.

During it's first hunting season try to let the dog see other retrievers at work. When you have the opportunity to hunt with a companion and a second dog, let your pup watch the other dog make a retrieve before sending it for a retrieve of it's own. This will heighten your pup's retrieving desire. When your pup sees a bird

Once a young retriever has learned obedience commands and been force-trained to retrieve, he's ready to go hunting. A full season of hunting will boost his enthusiasm for his job and get him ready for the hard job of learning to handle.

fall and has marked the spot, release it quickly and send it for the retrieve. If the fall is more difficult and the pup is not sure where the bird fell, walk the dog at heel into the vicinity of the fall and then release it and share the search saying, "fetch, fetch" as you work upwind and across the wind looking for the bird. The pup will learn to use it's nose and to hunt for cripples faster if you go out and help it search.

Don't teach retrievers hand signals too early. They should have one full season of actual hunting and retrieving before you teach them to handle. They've got to learn to hunt for fallen birds and learn how to find them. Teaching handling too early makes dogs reliant on being handled to where the bird is and their own hunting skills go undeveloped. The dog has to learn to hunt and use his nose and should be delivering to hand before any handling is taught.

During the dog's first season make things easy for him. Let him see the fallen bird, then send him quickly to make the retrieve.

There is no end of new things for a hunting retriever to learn. This Golden know how to save her energy for the hunt and prefers to ride across the flooded rice field of Louisiana on a four-wheeler.

(17)

The Perfect Delivery

Delivery to hand is a mark of a good hunting retriever not just because it looks nice but because you don't want your dog trotting all over the place carrying your ducks or dropping them halfway between the water and the blind and making you have to go out and pick them up. The dog's job is to bring the duck all the way to you and hold it gently until you take it from it's mouth.

Field trials require that the dog sit at your side to deliver and there's nothing wrong with that. But when you are in a duck blind the dog can't very well sit at your side to deliver unless you are going to go out of the blind to accept the duck. Forget it! When you are hunting you'll want the dog to deliver in a variety of ways. Sometimes it will be bringing a goose back to the edge of a pit blind and you'll be reaching up from underground to take it from the dog's mouth. Or you'll be in a duck blind with a little door at one end and it will be enough for the dog to bring the duck to the doorway where you can reach out from your seat and take it. In a duck boat you'll find it best to take the duck from the dog's mouth when it swims up and first puts it's feet on the gunwale. When you're hunting the important thing is not sitting to deliver, but delivering to hand.

Sitting to deliver isn't necessary, but it's good manners and guarantees that you will get a delivery to hand and not have a duck dropped at the water's edge.

In hunting retriever tests dogs are not required to sit to deliver but they are expected to go directly to their handlers with no wandering around and to hold the duck gently until it is taken from their mouths. Whether they sit beside or in front of the handler, or deliver standing up for that matter, doesn't count against them, so long as the delivery is direct and to hand.

However, the funny thing is that the best way to get a good quick direct delivery to hand is to train your dog to finish his delivery by sitting at your side if the situation permits it. Even though you will accept delivery to hand in whatever manner seems best when you're hunting, those deliveries will be cleaner if you require the dog to sit to deliver in training sessions.

You will want the dog to sit and deliver on the same side you have taught it to heel — the side on which you do not carry your gun.

The best way to teach the dog this maneuver is to have it drag a short line during retrieving lessons. When the dog is approaching carrying the dummy reach out and grab the line and use it to steer

A sitting delivery looks nice and is a good indicator of the control a handler has over his dog. This Chesapeake's manners are perfect whether he is hunting or in the training field.

[97]

When a sitting delivery is not practical, let the bars down and accept delivery to hand without disturbing the hunt by climbing out of the blind. Dogs learn to retrieve to hand whether sitting or standing outside the blind.

the dog around in a tight turn on the delivery side. As it completes the turn and comes even with your knee, order it to sit and pull up on the line. Then reach across the dog's face and always take the dummy from the far side of its mouth. This will cause the dog to turn it's head towards you slightly as you accept completion of the retrieve and will accomplish the aim of having the dog put the dummy in your hand.

If the dog veers to the wrong side of you when it is approaching with the dummy, step out to block it, grab the dragging line and draw the dog firmly to the correct side before steering it through a tight turn and saying "*sit.*" This will prevent the dog from circling behind you to come up on the delivery side.

A clean sitting delivery looks good. It's a mark of the dog's trainability. Your insistence that these manners be followed when possible will result in more direct deliveries to hand even when sitting to deliver is impractical during real hunts.

Step back as the dog sits to deliver. This will cause the dog to turn it's head towards you and complete the delivery to hand with perfect manners.

(18)

Steadying Without Force

Steadiness in retriever lingo means that the dog will sit still until sent to make a retrieve regardless of what distractions may tempt him to break and rush out before he is ordered to go. While hunters talk and joke in the blind waiting for ducks to appear the dog must sit steadily. When ducks are sighted and duck calls come into use and hunters reposition themselves for the shot, the dog must be steady. When the birds come sailing into range the dog's steadiness is tested even more and when the hunters scramble to their feet and throw guns to their shoulders and salvos of shots are fired and ducks fall from the sky and hit the ground and water with exciting thumps and splashes, the dog's steadiness undergoes the greatest test of all. Still it must wait, remaining steady as its handler lays down his gun, shuffles out of the blind and lines the dog up to retrieve the duck he wants brought in first. The dog must remain steady until it is sent to go.

If it were not so, if dogs were free to dash out whenever they thought there was something out there to retrieve, your days in duck blinds would be unsettling, to say the least. How long would it be before a dog leaped out into someone's line of fire as he swung with a low-flying bird? What would happen if the dog smashed against you in a drive to

The young Lab at left is learning that a retrieve is a reward he gets for being steady. If he moves, the other dog gets the retrieve and he gets a rap from the training stick.

get a duck just as you were rising to shoot and nudging your safety off? Steadiness is a requirement based on safety, not just nice manners.

Teaching steadiness is easier if you bring the dog up expecting to wait to be sent before it goes out to retrieve. The only times you should let a dog rush out to retrieve without being sent is when you are trying to buoy the spirits of a dog that isn't sure retrieving is fun. As long as the dog is hot to retrieve, hold it back until you give the command to *fetch*.

The traditional means of breaking a retriever to steadiness involves force and that will be explained farther on. But there is another method which has more to do with manipulating the dog's mind and it is marvelously effective.

This is a method which was first demonstrated to me by professional trainer Ron Mathis of Pontchahoa Kennels, Husser, Louisiana. I have used it since and believe me, this is the way to go. By this method dogs learn that retrieves are rewards they get for being steady and once they get that message they steady themselves in order to get more retrieves. It relies on the natural

[102]

canine sense of jealousy and it gets into a dog's mind to a degree that far surpasses fear of punishment.

You need a helper and another dog, preferably a steady one. Have the two dogs sit about ten feet apart. You keep your dog leashed and stand beside it with a training stick poised over his back. When your dog is ready, nod to the helper. He shoots a gun and throws a dummy out in front of the dogs. If your dog so much as lifts his fanny off the ground, rap him across the rump with the stick and order him to *sit*. When he is seated, nod again to the helper who then sends the steady dog to make the retrieve. If your dog, out of jealousy, rises to his feet when the steady dog is sent out, jerk him back down into a sitting position and rap him across the rump until he responds.

Repeat this procedure as many times as necessary giving the steady dog the retrieves each time your dog moves with the intention of breaking. If your dog moves, the steady dog is sent for

When your dog is first being steadied tie it to a stout post or tree leaving some slack in a short tether. Then throw dummies and birds and shoot. When the dog breaks it will be snubbed when it hits the end of the rope. Use a spiked chain slip collar for stubborn dogs that need extra convincing.

Shooting flyers in front of the dogs is the ultimate steadying test. If the Lab at left stays steady, he will get the retrieve. If he breaks he'll get a whack with the training stick and the steady Chesapeake at right will get the retrieve. Jealousy will help steady the young dog.

the retrieve and your dog is jerked back into a sitting position and rapped with the training stick. Eventually, your dog will try sitting still when the dummy is thrown out. When that happens, send him quickly for the retrieve and make the steady dog honor. Give your pup a lot of "good boy" talk when he brings the dummy to you. Have him sit. Repeat the throw immediately. As soon as your dog understands that when it moves the other dog gets the retrieve, you will see gratifying results and the seed of steadiness will begin to germinate. Once he realizes he only gets to retrieve when he is steady, your dog will begin to steady himself.

As training proceeds you will have to increase the level of distraction. Throw birds instead of dummies. Shoot multiple shots instead of just one. Blow duck calls. Throw doubles. Do whatever is necessary to raise the level of distraction to the point where your dog breaks, and when it does, send the other dog for the retrieve. If you apply this method consistently, always giving the other dog the retrieve when your dog offers to break, a very deeply rooted habit of steadiness will be built.

If you don't have a steady retriever to use as the second dog in this training procedure you can get away with having the helper keep the second dog leashed until it is sent to retrieve. The steadiness of the second dog is not as crucial as your dog's understanding that it only gets the reward of the retrieve when it stays seated and doesn't move until you send it, no matter what distractions occur.

This is a positive approach to steadying. All other methods are negative, involving punishing the dog when he breaks rather than rewarding it when it is steady.

Using Force

Traditionally, retrievers have been steadied by attaching a fifteen foot line to the dog's chain collar and securing the other end to a

Steadying a dog is one thing, keeping it steady takes more work. Here the trainer works one dog while two other steady dogs are required to watch and wait their turn.

[105]

Steadying a stubborn retriever requires that you tempt him to break, then correct him with whatever degree of force is required. Keep increasing the level of temptation that the dog will overcome and correct it with force when it does break. It is kinder to get the job done once and for all than to keep hacking at the dog for the rest of its life.

sturdy post. The dog is tricked into breaking and hurts itself when it hits the end of the line. When it learns not to run out and hit the end of the line the trainer takes the line in hand and jerks the dog back into a sitting position as soon as it rises up and indicates its intent to break when a dummy or bird is thrown. Whips, pellet guns, sling shots and electronic collars are all used to punish dogs in the act of breaking so that they will remain steady out of fear of punishment. Some dogs require much more force and more extreme punishment depending upon the degree of their stubbornness in resisting the trainer's efforts to gain ultimate control.

The Mathis method, on the other hand, involves no force. The training stick is used simply to remind the dog to sit, not to beat him. The dog's punishment for trying to break is simply denial of the retrieve. But when it stays steady it gets the retrieve as a reward for proper behavior and even the toughest dogs submit to their natural jealousy and become steady rather than letting the other dog have the retrieve.

Steadying In a Boat

Once your dog is steady in situations on land, it's a good idea to also steady it in a boat. It must understand that steadiness is required in every situation it may encounter when actually hunting. The easiest way to steady a dog in a boat is to put your duck boat up on saw horses and seat the dog in its place in the boat with a short tether attached from the dog's collar to a solid part of the boat's structure.

Do whatever is necessary to tempt the dog into breaking. When it does dive over the side before being sent it will be fetched up short by the tether and will find itself hanging in midair by the neck. Don't be in a great hurry to rescue the dog. Let the lesson sink in for a moment before you turn it loose. Then immediately repeat the procedure. Few dogs will fail to grasp the idea quickly. When it does stay steady, send the dog for the retrieve and give lavish praise when it is completed.

Chad Driskill uses a stump to instill the idea that a dog must not creep or move about when the shooting starts. The stump gives the dog a sense of place. If it moves from that place it will be shocked with the electronic training collar. Working the dog from a training box teaches the same concept.

To steady a dog in a boat put your boat up on sawhorses and tie the dog on a short lead in the bow. Then shoot and throw dummies tempting the dog to break. When it bails out over the side it will fetch up short and be left hanging. A couple of such episodes is all it takes to teach most dogs to stay still in a boat until they are ordered out.

The electronic training collar is useful in steadying. The dog has been trained to sit on command or whistle signal. If it breaks when a dummy is thrown, the handler will transmit a low intensity shock through the collar unit the dog wears on its back. The dog soon learns it must stay until sent to retrieve no matter what happens out front.

(19)

Lining Lessons For Retrievers

No matter how well a retriever has been trained to mark where birds fall, there will be times when the dog must be sent after birds that fell out of its sight. To make these *blind* retrieves effectively, the dog must be taught to run out in a straight line to distant points.

Training retrievers to run out straight in the direction you send them is called *lining*. You train them to take the line indicated by your hand and to run out straight in that direction until they find the bird or dummy you have hidden out there. *Lining* depends upon the dog learning to trust your hand. Once it knows and accepts the fact that there is always something to retrieve out in the direction your hand indicates, the dog will begin to trust your hand and will become increasingly precise in running straight in the direction you send it.

This trust is built by making absolutely sure that the dog always finds something when it takes the line you send it out on.

The most effective lining drill I have ever seen is that used by professional hunting retriever trainer Ron Mathis of Pontchahoa Kennels in Husser, Louisiana. Ron uses a system he calls the Wagon Wheel to teach dogs to run accurate lines for long distances with

Ron Mathis uses the Wagon Wheel pattern to teach dogs to take lines. He starts with dummies at four points of the compass and adds dummies in between as the dog learns to differentiate between which dummy it is being sent to retrieve. Distances are increased as the dog's proficiency grows.

absolute trust in the direction he indicates with his hand.

You can use this drill in its simplest form to start young retrievers and can build on the Wagon Wheel method as the dog's abilities progress throughout its training. Simple to understand and dependable in the results it produces, the Wagon Wheel method can be expanded to suit the ability level of any retriever. Here's how it works.

"You start with just four dummies," Ron Mathis explains. "With the dog sitting at your side you throw a dummy out about ten feet in front of him. Use a short lead to prevent the dog from running out for it. With the dog sitting at your side, turn 90 degrees in a clockwise direction, patting your thigh to get the dog to turn with you, and throw the second dummy ten feet in front of him. Then turn another 90 degrees keeping him sitting but having him turn to face the same direction you are facing and throw out the third dummy. Turn another 90 degrees and throw out the fourth. You now have dummies at 12 o'clock, 3 o'clock, 6 o'clock and 9 o'clock.

Next face the dog towards the 12 o'clock dummy and indicate it with your hand. With your hand in front of the dog's nose and just above the level of its eyes, indicate the line you want it to take and send the dog for the dummy saying, *"Back!"*

When the dog dives out, grabs the dummy and returns to you, make it sit beside you and deliver to hand. Give lavish praise. Then attach the leash and, with the dog sitting beside you, throw the dummy back to it's 12 o'clock position. Use the leash and the sit command to prevent the dog from following the thrown dummy. Then turn clockwise to face the 3 o'clock dummy, patting your thigh to get the dog to turn with you. When the dog is sitting facing the 3 o'clock dummy indicate the line with your hand and send him for that dummy using the *"Back!"* command. Repeat this procedure with each dummy, working in a clockwise direction. As you continue the drill the dog will be learning to ignore the dummy you throw back and to concentrate on the one you turn towards and indicate with your hand that you want retrieved.

Since the dog can see all four dummies lying in plain sight, it is

Start with dummies in plain sight at short distance, then increase the distances as the dog becomes proficient at going out for the dummy you indicate with your hand.

When positioning a dog to go out on a line indicated by your hand, look from his tail up its spine and out through its head. Don't send the dog BACK until it is lined up like this.

easy for it to comprehend that you are using your hand to indicate which dummy is to be picked up. It is important also that you turn the dog to face the dummy you indicate with your hand so that its body is lined up to move out in that direction. Your dog will quickly comprehend this drill and become confident and happy during the lesson as it progresses.

As the lessons continue you can begin to mix up the order in which you send the dog for retrieves. Work him around the four dummies in a clockwise direction and then back around the circle in a counterclockwise direction. Then start mixing up the order, turning the dog 180 degrees from the 12 o'clock dummy, say, to the 6 o'clock dummy, from the 9 o'clock to the 3 o'clock, and so forth.

Once the dog is happily dashing out to pick up whichever dummy you line him towards, it is time to start lengthening the distances. Instead of throwing dummies out ten feet, throw them twenty feet, forty feet, sixty feet. Gradually increase the distances until the dog will race out a hundred yards or more in a straight line to scoop up the dummy to which you give a line.

Now start adding more spokes to the wheel. If you consider the lines to the four original dummies as four spokes of a wheel, you next add spokes halfway between the original four. At first you will have to make the new spokes short ones. Send the dog out for its normal long retrieve on the 12 o'clock line, then give him the line to a new dummy which you have tossed in plain sight halfway between the 12 o'clock and the 3 o'clock. Then send him for a long retrieve on the three o'clock line. Keep the new spokes short at first so that the dog can see the new dummies that have been added. As he becomes skilled at following the lines you give him to the various dummies you can gradually lengthen the new spokes until the dog will take long straight lines to whichever dummy you face him towards and indicate with your hand.

This dog's head is lined up with the trainer's hand but it's spine indicates it will run out to the left of the correct line. The dog should be repositioned before being sent.

When giving a dog a line, keep your hand above the dog's line of sight and just in front of its head. The dog's vision must not be blocked by your hand, but the hand should appear in the top of the dog's sight picture as a clear indicator of the direction you want followed.

During these lessons it is important *not* to stop the dog with the *sit whistle* or attempt to redirect it to the line you wish followed by giving hand signals if the dog takes an incorrect line. Instead, whenever the dog starts off on the wrong line, simply say *NO* and call it back to your side and start again. This lesson should be confined to drilling on running out on correct lines and should not be confused by mixing in hand signals at this point.

"We use the Wagon Wheel strictly for lining practice," Ron Mathis explains. "The point is to teach the dog to line itself up with your body and follow the line you indicate with your hand for longer and longer distances. We are convincing the dog that there is always something to retrieve somewhere out on that line. As you add more spokes you are refining the dog's ability to concentrate on the line."

At first Mathis lets the dog see him throw each dummy out into position, but as the distances are lengthened a point is reached where it is no longer possible to throw the dummies back into place after each retrieve. At that point he starts each drill session by walking out and scattering groups of dummies at the end of each spoke. Once the dog sees that there are several dummies at each location it will comprehend that the important thing is to run straight out on the line you indicate and bring back a dummy from the correct group. If the dog veers offline or switches to the wrong group of dummies, Mathis stops it with a firm *NO*, calls the dog and repeats the line.

As the distances become longer an electronic training collar is useful. The collar gives you the ability to stop the dog at any distance if it veers off the line or switches to the wrong group of dummies. If the dog is consistently stopped and called back in to try again on the same line it will soon recognize that running straight out on the line is *safe*, and results in finding a dummy to retrieve, whereas departure from the line always brings correction and necessitates being called in and starting over. Dogs trained by this method become masters at running very long lines perfectly straight with practice.

Right from the start the dog's trust in your hand is being reinforced every time it takes the correct line and is rewarded by finding a dummy where you indicated it would be. Finding the dummy and completing the retrieve is the reward the dog gets for taking the correct line and as the dog's trust in your hand develops it will dash out with increasing enthusiasm, knowing that a dummy waits out there to be retrieved.

"This is a positive experience for the dog," Mathis explains. "It's important to give the dog confidence by praising it each time it does right. Keep the dog's spirit up and encourage it with a lot of 'good dog' talk."

There is no end to what you can do with this drill. As the dog's ability level increases Mathis adds new twists. He may, for instance, give the dog a line which goes between two dummies which are in plain sight but leads to a distant unseen dummy. As the dog's trust in his hand grows he stops using all the spokes of the wagon wheel and instead uses just a segment of the wheel with dummies hidden at varying distances on lines which lie at closer angles to one another.

In advanced training, Mathis mixes in diversions. He may, for instance, use a bird releaser to pop a bird into the air and have the dog mark it, then turn the dog and give it a line to a distant unseen dummy which was planted earlier. When you can get the dog to mark a bird it saw fall and turn with you to take the line you indicate toward an unseen dummy instead, you have developed the dog's trust in your hand to a very high degree.

Most trainers find it helps to have one special place where lining drills are carried out. They mark the spots where distant dummies are placed with small plastic flags so that they will know exactly where the dummies are and can give the dog accurate lining indications. By working the dog on the same course day after day the lines become established in the dog's mind and it more clearly comprehends what is required as the distances are increased.

Eventually, lining practice will be moved away from the established course and done in random places. But, when problems occur, you can always take the dog back to the established course for reminder drilling. The Wagon Wheel drill is a most effective method for teaching retrievers to run straight when sent out to make blind retrieves.

Lining the Dog Up Right

You can tell the direction your dog is going to run out in by looking at the way it is sitting. When you are setting the dog up to be *lined* from your side to a distant fall, look from its tail, up through its spine

When lining in water begin by working the dog from the water's edge. Later you can move back a few steps at a time as the dog learns to stay on the same line whether on land or water.

and out over its head. That's the line the dog is going to take, so be sure that it is also the line you want it to take before you send it *back*.

If the dog is lined up wrong you can reposition it by heeling it away from the starting point in a tight circle and bring it back to the spot in line with the direction you will send it. Don't give the *back* command unless the dog's spine is straight and it's head is pointed in the correct direction.

Lining in Water

Lining drills in water can be done the same way as on land. Using just a part of the Wagon Wheel pattern, throw dummies on the water in a fan pattern with lots of space between. Start with short throws and keep the dummies widely spaced until the dog gets the hang of it and then gradually lengthen the distance the dog must swim.

At the same time, gradually move the starting line back from the water's edge so that the dog learns to run straight on the line you indicate to the edge of the water and then continue swimming on that line to the correct dummy.

An ideal situation is to train at a small pond where you can hide the dummies in cover on the shore and work the dog from the opposite side.

Once your dog becomes proficient at lining in water, take him out in your duck boat and work him in open water on a lake, lining the dog to dummies that you have dropped at greater and greater distances.

As long as you start with short retrieves and gradually lengthen the distance the dog must swim, your dog will respond by going the extra distance. Dogs that have not had this gradual increase will never understand the concept of swimming long distances in straight lines and you will not be able to go out far enough for blind retrieves on water when ducks are down that the dog did not see fall.

Lining drills are important on both land and water. You want your dog to go out on the line you indicate until it either finds a bird or dummy or is stopped with a whistle and sent in another direction by hand signals. This takes lots of practice in many different locations, but the whole secret to success is in starting short and gradually increasing the distance the dog must take the line.

(20)

Training Retrievers To Handle

Teaching retrievers to handle should be delayed until the dog has a full season of hunting and simple retrieving behind it. You want to have your dog really burning to retrieve before you start making it obey hand signals. Teaching your dog to handle means teaching it to go *back* or *over* to the left or right in response to your hand and whistle signals. It is a sobering experience and may become tiresome to a dog that has not had it's retrieving desire kindled first.

Knowing when to handle is important. You don't want to overhandle your dog or it will lose initiative and look to you for direction rather than using it's nose; yet if it is not taught to handle the dog will hunt out of control and you won't be able to direct it to unmarked falls.

The best guide for when to handle that I have seen is the one used by Omar Driskill. He holds up two fingers in a "V" at arm's length and puts the place he wants the dog to go in the middle. If the dog is outside the "V", it needs to be stopped with a *sit whistle* and handled. If it's within the "V" he does not interfere as long as the dog is hunting enthusiastically.

The Back Cast

"*Back*" is the hardest handling command for dogs to learn. *Come in,* and *overs* to the left and right are easier, so it's a good idea to get your dog doing *backs* well before adding the other directional commands.

Start with the dog facing you about ten yards away. Blow the *sit whistle* to anchor the dog in place and then throw a dummy over its head so that it lands out in back of the dog. Snap your fingers to make the dog look at you. If the dog is not sitting facing you blow the *come in* whistle and have it take a few steps towards you. Then stop it with the *sit whistle*. Now, with the dog facing you, throw one arm straight up in the air and say "*back!*"

When the dog completes the retrieve have it sit. Then you walk away in another direction for ten yards or so and then throw the dummy back over the dog so that it lands beyond the dog in this new direction. Keep changing your positions this way so that the dog gets to understand that "*back*" means it should run straight away from you no matter where you are standing when you give the command.

Now start building on this knowledge. Use two dummies. When the dog is running out to retrieve the one you threw behind it, turn and throw the second dummy a few yards in the opposite direction.

After the dog retrieves the first dummy you will leave it sitting and walk off a few yards and then give it a "*back*" towards the second unseen dummy. If the dog takes your command and goes back it will find the dummy it didn't know you threw and it's understanding of the command will be deepened. It will learn that there is always something to retrieve in the direction you send it. Keep repeating this lesson in constantly changing positions until the dog gets good at it every time. Then begin lengthening the throws and increasing the distance between you and the dog when you give the command.

Remember, the dog must be facing you when you give the command. If it is not you can reposition it by calling it a few steps towards you and then stopping it with the *sit whistle*. Always be sure to give the *back* command from a point on a line from the dog to the dummy so that a run straight back away from you will make the dog succeed. Keep distances very short at first and lengthen them as the dog's understanding develops.

[120]

Make your hand signals clear. When signalling BACK, throw your whole body into it, reaching high and throwing your arm straight up.

Once the dog will reliably take the *"back"* command to dummies it did not see fall, it's time to start teaching casts to right and left.

Start at very short distances. With the dog sitting facing you, throw a dummy a few yards to the right, then send the dog, saying *"over"* as you give an exaggerated arm motion to the right. If done at a short distance the dog will probably respond to this new command the first time it hears it. If it balks, give the arm signal and say *"fetch,* over" a few times until the dog gets the idea. Then drop the *"fetch"* and proceed using only the *"over"* command in combination with the arm signal.

Once the dog understands that *"over"* and the arm signal mean it's released to go, switch from *overs* on the right to *overs* on the left for a few throws at very short distance. Now the dog knows that *"over"* means it is to make a retrieve, but it has not yet learned to differentiate between right and left. That's the next step.

You can teach the dog to differentiate right from left most easily by placing dummies in two groups about twenty feet apart. Have the dog walk at heel beside you as you lay three dummies in one group and walk off twenty feet and lay down a group of three others. Then heel the dog to a position halfway between the two groups and blow the *sit whistle.*

With the dog sitting facing you between the two groups of dumies, you then back up a few steps. Snap your fingers to get the dog to look at you and when you have it's attention, say *"over"* and point with a fully extended arm to one of the groups of dummies. Done at short distance, the dog should understand your meaning and dive for one of the dummies you pointed to. When it completes the delivery, walk the dog back to it's position between the two groups and repeat the procedure, only this time send it to the other group of dummies. Begin at very short distances, literally only a few feet, and build the distance as the dog's understanding increases.

If the dog gets confused and runs in the wrong direction, stop it with the *sit whistle,* walk out to it and heel the dog back to its center position. Then bring the dummies closer before you repeat the cast.

[122]

The OVER hand signal should be accompanied by a step in the direction indicated by your hand. This will help convey the meaning of the command.

Handling lessons should begin at short distances and the distance is gradually lengthened as the dog's confidence grows. Eventually the dog will take hand signals at any distance that is within sight of the handler.

Switching

Sometimes a dog will run to the correct group of dummies, then turn and dash off towards the other group, with or without a dummy in its mouth. If that happens stop the dog either with the *sit whistle* or by running out and grabbing it and make it complete the first retrieve and then heel it back to the center and make it wait to be sent for the second. Stay in a position from which you can intercept the dog if it switches from one group to the other.

At this stage give the dog an *over* to one side, then an *over* to the other and so on using two groups of dummies that are in plain sight. This makes the dog concentrate on differentiating between the two groups and going to the one you indicate. Three or four retrieves to each side are ample for one session.

It's still too early to mix *overs* and *backs* in the same exercise, but you don't want the dog to forget how to perform the *back* command

[124]

while you are teaching it *overs*. So, after the *over* lesson, pick up the dummies and give the dog three or four *backs* with no other dummies on the ground to confuse things.

Keep *overs* and *backs* separated in the training sessions until the dog fully understands the meaning of each command and can be sent in the correct direction even when you have backed up fifty or sixty yards from the seated dog and can send it fifty or sixty yards right or left to visible groups of dummies.

Mixing Overs and Backs

When you first start mixing *overs* and *backs,* the dog may have a tendency to go right or left when you send it *back*. This tendency can be avoided if you anticipate it and make it easier for the dog to succeed.

Start by sending the dog for three simple *backs* to dummies you throw behind it. Then put the dog on sit facing you and throw a dummy to its right, one to its left and, finally, one behind the dog. The dog will alays want to pick up the last dummy you threw first, so start by letting him. Send him for the *back* first. After the delivery is completed, heel the dog to a position between the two remaining dummies and have it retrieve them as *overs*. Repeat this several times so that the dog recognizes that there are three dummies involved, but always throw the *back* dummy last and let the dog pick it up first.

Next, proceed from thrown dummies to groups of dummies which you let the dog watch you lay out on the ground. Lay out groups of three dummies to the right, left and behind the point at which the dog will sit. Start at very short distances. Send the dog for a *back* first, then an *over* to each pile and then a *back* again until all nine dummies are picked up.

If the dog goes the wrong direction on any command, stop it with the *sit whistle,* call the dog to you, heel it back to the starting place and try again. By starting at very short distances and gradually lengthening them as the dog's proficiency improves you will be able to stay in control of the situation and can help the dog succeed by using lots of body language as you give the hand signals. Keep the dog's spirit up with lots of "good boy" talk each time the dog does right and don't lose your temper when the dog goes the wrong way.

[125]

When you are really hunting you won't always be able to get out of the blind and stand beside the dog to send it for a retrieve. This dog has a good mark on a fallen bird and needs only to be ordered BACK and given a wave of a hand. He knows his job and needs no further help this time.

Just keep your whistle in your mouth and be ready to blow it and make the dog stop and sit before it compounds the error by running far in the wrong direction. Then take it back to the starting place and try again. Whenever things go wrong, shorten the distance. When the dog is doing well, increase the distance step by step.

Precise handling is the result of lots of practice. A retriever is never finished with handling practice. Advanced forms of this basic drill will be the meat of practice training sessions for the rest of your dog's life.

(21)

Creative Fencing For Retriever Training

Teaching dogs to run a straight line when given a hand signal by a distant handler has always been a sticky training problem. Dogs often start off in the right direction, but then hook into a curving course that takes them off the line you are trying to put them on and they wind up wandering all over the place.

Paul and Barbara Genthner keep dogs running straight on "*over*" and "*back*" commands by the creative use of fencing on their training area. Once the dog gets in the habit of hewing to a straight course because the fence prevents him from doing otherwise, it becomes easier to keep him straight.

A line of woven wire fencing with a gate in the center and a right angle corner at one end is a good set-up for working on several important handling lessons.

With the gate closed and the dog sitting with his back to the fence and facing you, give him "*over*" commands to piles of dummies you have placed on his left and right. To get him to run straighter on his "*back*" commands, you can work parallel to the fence, gradually increasing the distance between you and the dog when you give the command and also increasing the distance he must run to the dummy.

Paul and Barbara Genthner of Tealbrook Kennels, Monticello, Fla. use gates and fences in a variety of ways to teach dogs to handle, avoid switching and confine their hunting areas.

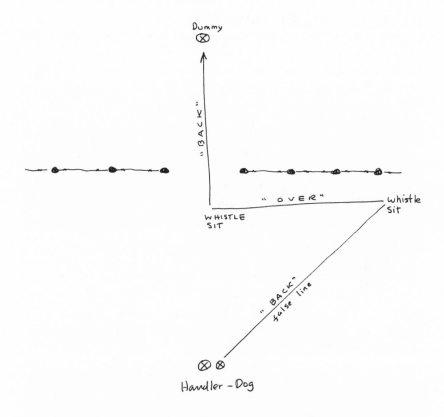

Dummy

"BACK"

"OVER"

WHISTLE
SIT

whistle
sit

"BACK"
false line

Handler - Dog

Handler sends dog on a false line to the fence, stops it with a whistle, then sends it on an "over" to the left. Dog is stopped with whistle in front of the gate, then sent "Back" through the gate to the dummy. Fence and gate make it easier for the dog to understand what is being required.

When the dog knows the meaning of the *"over"* and *back"* commands and is obeying them crisply, it is ready to be handled to a bird or dummy by the use of both commands given in sequence.

At this point the Genthners work with the fence gate open. The set up calls for having handler and dog together at a point opposite the open gate and the bird an equal distance through the gate on the other side of the fence.

The handler initially sends the dog on a *false* line towards the fence wall to the right of the gate. When the dog nears the fence the dog is stopped by a whistle and given an *"over"* to the left, parallel to the fence. When it reaches the gate the dog is again stopped with a whistle and is now given a *"back"* command through the open gate to the bird.

"You can mix this up and send the dog to either side of the gate for practice on both *overs* to right and left, and gradually increase all the distances," says Paul. The fence line keeps the dog from "hooking" and he'll learn to do his *"overs"* nice and straight.

Switching

The Genthners also use a fence line to straighten out dogs that switch from one dummy to another when doubles are thrown. The handler sends the dog down either side to dummies that are thrown on opposite sides of the fence.

"It's a simple trick but it prevents a dog from picking up one bird and then running over to the second before retrieving the first," Paul explains. "The fence makes "switching" impossible so the dog gets in the habit of completing the first retrieve and then being sent out for the second. Again, distances are gradually increased.

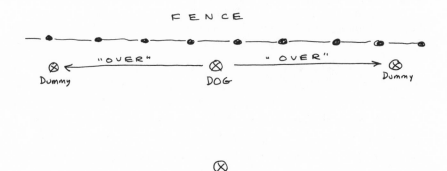

Working the dog from a spot where its back is against a fence help the dog learn to run straight to right or left on "overs".

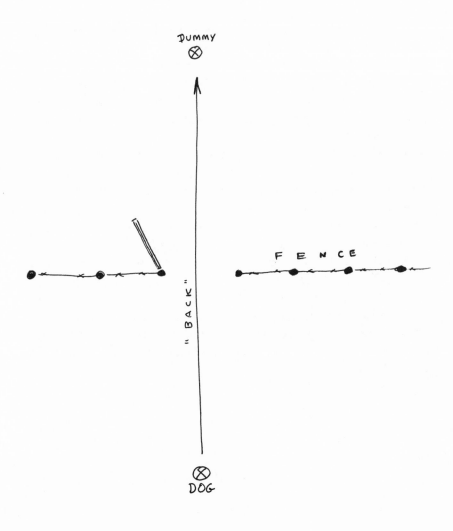

Working the dog through an open gate will help it learn to run straight when given the "back" command.

When a retriever won't stay in one area and hunt for a fallen bird, but wants to go on and hunt in wider and wider circles, the Genthners head for the fence again. This time they use a fence corner and place the bird inside the "V" of the fence. They work the dog into the "V" where the fence restricts him from hunting out wider and wider and instead forces him to stay in the area and really hunt for the bird.

"We use this when a dog tends to veer off line on long falls," Paul explained. "The fences keep it from getting completely off course and restrict its hunting to the area where the bird really is. Once it has found a few this way, the dog learns to hunt more diligently and not just run around. You can't handle your dog to every fall because in hunting situations the bird isn't always where you may think it is. Retriever gundogs must learn to stay and hunt in the area where they are sent."

One other training gimmick that uses a little woven wire fencing is a three-sided woven wire blind, all brushed in like a hunting blind. "We work gundogs out of wire blinds to teach them to go out the open end and not through the wall or over the top," Paul noted. If you have ever seen a retriever go through the side of a blind or had one climb out over you and your loaded gun, you'll fully understand the wisdom of this training detail.

A line of fence between two piles of dummies prevents dogs from switching on doubles. Dogs develop the habit of returning straight to the handler without investigating other nearby dummies. Trainer uses right or left hand to indicate which way dog is to turn on "Back" command.

(22)

The Retrieve-R-Trainer

There is one gadget which has proven to be tremendously effective among retriever trainers. Appropriately patented as the Retrieve-R-Trainer, this tool fires a retrieving dummy up to 80 yards using .22 caliber blanks as the propellant. The device was invented by Art Johnson of Silver Springs, Maryland. The earliest prototype fired beverage cans into the air for shotgun target practice. Later the device was modified to shoot retrieving dummies and quickly became popular among retriever trainers.

One of its earliest uses is in introducing a young dog to the sound of a gun. When you consider that dogs should first hear gunfire when they are distracted by something else (chasing a bird or butterfly, for example) the Retrieve-R-Trainer fills the bill. Using a light load which makes little noise, you shoot a dummy a short distance. The pup hears the shot but is distracted and excited by seeing the dummy fly at the same instant he hears the crack of the gun. Do this when the pup is running a little distance from you and he will be excited rather than being frightened by the sound. Later you shorten the distance and, later still, increase the load. The dog learns to accept gunfire as a signal that means there is something to retrieve.

Although the Retrieve-R-Trainer enables a man to shoot a dummy three or four times as far as a dummy can be thrown by hand, its essential value is not only for distance. The length of the shot can be adjusted by the degree to which the dummy is slid onto the barrel of the device. Slip it on just a bit and you get a short shot. The farther the dummy is slid onto the barrel, the longer the shot will be.

In early retrieving training short shots are advisable, so that the dog sees exactly where the dummy lands. Later you increase the distance, thereby developing the dog's ability to mark the spot where the dummy falls. The dog's memory can be developed by shooting several dummies from the same location before sending him to retrieve. He learns to remember that two or three dummies have been fired out and thinks harder about where they fell.

In advanced work, the Retrieve-R-Trainer is used for planting dummies across water, or for planting distant "blind" falls in which the dog does not see the dummy fired, but is sent to locate it by hand signals.

Steadying relies on the trainer's ability to tempt a dog to break so that you have an opportunity to correct him. You want the dog to break, in other words, so that you can correct him.

With the Retrieve-R-Trainer you have a good tool with which to tempt the dog to break. Once you have picked up the checkcord, fire the Retrieve-R-Trainer. The sound of the gun and the dummy whizzing through the air will surely cause the dog to break and give you a chance to bust him. Teaching the dog to stop when a shot is fired and then tempting him to break by firing the Retrieve-R-Trainer again establishes the dog's understanding of the stop to shot requirement and makes it that much easier to steady him when real birds are used.

A hunting retriever should stop when a bird flushes. Teaching gundogs to stop to flush is made easier using the Retrieve-R-Trainer in "walk-up" situations. With the dog quartering ahead, fire off a dummy and instantly stop the dog with a checkcord. Then walk up to him and send him for the retrieve. He'll soon learn that he is to stop when he hears the gun and sees a dummy in the air.

This same unexpected firing of the Retrieve-R-Trainer can be used to teach a duck dog to sit and wait to be sent when he hears a gun go off and sees an object falling through the air. Such lessons can be taught on land or in a boat.

Trainer Ron Mathis has modified his Retrieve-R-Trainer by mounting it on a .22 caliber rifle stock. This extends its range and absorbs recoil better.

[135]

In many ways the Retrieve-R-Trainer doubles as a blank pistol, but it has a distinct advantage. Several states now rule that blank pistols must be registered as handguns and are not permitted to be brought into the state without proper permits. The Retrieve-R-Trainer, however, can travel anywhere without restriction, giving you the opportunity to take it with you on out-of-state trips on which you hope to do a little training.

Any adult can shoot the Retrieve-R-Trainer one-handed, provided you hold it properly. It is important to grip the handle so that the heel of your hand is facing away from your body. This enables your elbow to bend and absorb the mild recoil. If you hold your thumb towards the dummy, the recoil can cause your hand to slip and the back end of the Retrieve-R-Trainer can bark the skin.

Today the Retrieve-R-Trainer is produced by Specialty Products Corporation of Route 50, Box 158, Wye Mills, Maryland 21679. It is available through several dog supply catalogs, but is marketed chiefly through the Tidewater Specialties catalog which is published at the same address.

Constructed of high-grade steel and heavy-duty aluminum, the Retrieve-R-Trainer lasts for years if given regular cleaning and oiling.

Dummies are available in either canvas or high-density molded plastic foam, in highly visible blaze orange (which appears grey to dogs) and in white. The plastic dummies will shoot up to fifty percent farther than the canvas models.

(23)

Advanced Handling Drills

Now that your dog will take hand signals to the right, left and back from a position in front of you, it is time to begin teaching it to run back between two piles of dummies to retrieve from a third pile. Lay out the three piles of dummies in a triangle, but this time, instead of working from a point on the line between the right and left piles, bring the dog towards you a few feet. Then send it *back* to the rear pile so that it will have to cross the line between the side piles to make the retrieve. From now on keep backing up and increasing the distance between the dog's starting position and the crossline between the right and left dummy piles. When the dog gets confident about crossing the line between the right and left dummy piles to reach the rear pile, it is ready to move on to the Cross Pattern.

The Cross Pattern

You already have your dog working the upright line of the cross. You've been sending it back across the line between piles of dummies on the right and left to reach the pile in the rear when you give the *back* command and hand signal. Now you can start mixing *overs* and *backs* using the *sit whistle* to maintain control.

Start with the dog sitting facing you on the line between you and the rear pile of dummies. Using the hand signal and voice command, send the dog *back* to the rear pile. When it completes the retrieve, have the dog sit beside you and, using the *lining* hand gesture, send it *back* towards the rear dummy pile again. When the dog reaches the crossline between the right and left dummy piles, stop it with the *sit whistle* and send it *over* to one of the piles on the right or left.

Once the dog has completed this exercise successfully you can begin subsequent sessions working the dog from your side. *Line* it *back* to the crossline, stop it with the *sit whistle* and then send the dog *back* or *over* to the right or left in no particular order. Now your dog will be all attentiveness to see which way you are going to send it.

Some trainers find mowing crosspaths in the training field helps the dog run straight on *backs* and *overs* during early advanced handling sessions. Dummies are planted on the paths and distances are increased as the dog's confidence grows.

The Double Cross Pattern

Once your dog has mastered the cross pattern it has attained full comprehension of what hand signals mean. Now you can increase the challenge by increasing the length of the upright line of the cross pattern and adding a second crosspath. With dummies planted at the ends of the paths, you can send the dog *back* to either the first or second crosspath stop it with the *sit whistle* and subsequently send it *back* or *over* to the right or left dummy piles.

Penetrating Cover

Training is a matter of progressively increasing the level of distraction. When your dog is capable of following hand signals in an open field with mowed crosspaths your next step will be to repeat the same exercise in a different location where there are no

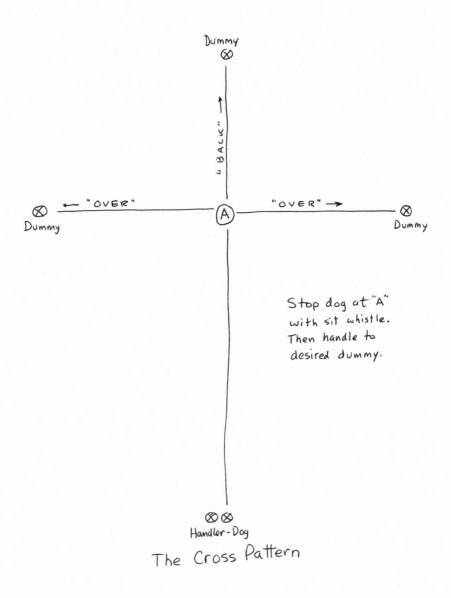

The Cross Pattern

Stop dog at "A" with sit whistle. Then handle to desired dummy.

The Cross and Double Cross Patterns are classic drills for advanced handling practice. As the dog's proficiency increases distances are increased and the drill is moved to heavier cover and water.

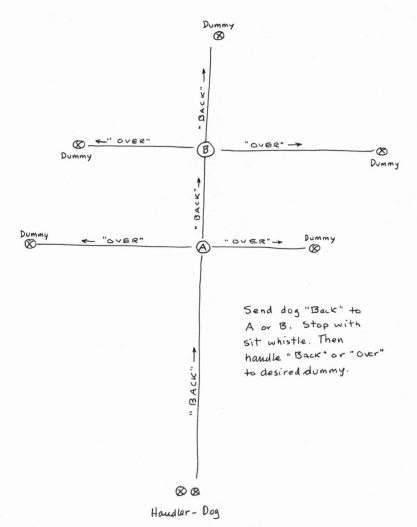

Send dog "Back" to
A or B. Stop with
sit whistle. Then
handle "Back" or "Over"
to desired dummy.

The Double Cross Pattern

crosspaths. Start working on the cross pattern through a band of heavy cover or a hedgerow. Will the dog go *back* through the hedge and stay on the line until you stop it with the *sit whistle?* Can you send it *over* through a patch of heavy cover? If not, start close and work at short distances again, with the dummy planted in plain sight on the far side of the cover. Keep adding natural obstacles and distractions as your dog's level of ability increases.

Mixed Lining and Handling

Be careful not to get hung up on *handling* to the extent that you neglect *lining* drills. Each training session at this stage of development should include both *handling* and *lining* exercises. A simple session which will keep the dog sharpened up can be accomplished with just two dummies. With the dog sitting beside you throw the dummies at right angles to one another. Be sure you remember where you throw each dummy. Then *line* the dog to one and when that is retrieved send the dog *back* on a false line, stop it with the *sit whistle* and give it an *over* to the second dummy. While the dog is running out for that one, throw the dummy you have in hand in another direction and be prepared to *line* the dog to that one next. You can progress around the training field in that fashion and give the dog a brisk brush-up on its skills in *lining* and *handling* before moving on to more challenging work.

Some Hints on Handling

Dogs tend to drift with the wind and the lay of the land. When you send your dog out on a *line* or give it a hand signal, remember that the dog will drift downwind and downhill and take that into consideration in choosing the line you will send it out on.

If a crosswind is blowing you should compensate for it by aiming the dog slightly upwind of the fall when you give it a line. Likewise, you should aim the dog slightly uphill from the actual point you want it to reach, to compensate for the dog's natural tendency to drift downhill on the outrun.

When you are handling your dog with *backs* and *overs* the same factors need to be remembered.

[141]

Using Electronic Collars

Advanced handling can be made very precise with proper use of the variable intensity electronic training collar. The dogs must first be taught the meaning of the commands and hand signals as has been described here, and should have been previously taught to come, and sit using electronic stimulation.

The electronic collar is now used to motivate an instant *whistle sit* when the dog is to be stopped and given a handling command. Electronic stimulation is then given simultaneously with *back* and *over* commands. The button is pressed at the instant the command is given and released as the dog moves out in the correct direction. If the dog takes the wrong directional line the button should be pressed simultaneously with the *sit whistle* and released the instant the dog sits, thus letting it succeed in stopping the stimulation by an obedient response.

By this technique low level electric stimulation is used in a positive way to motivate the dog to briskly obey commands which it fully understands. It is not used to punish the dog for an incorrect response. The electronic collar should not be used until the dog has been taught the meaning of commands by traditional methods.

(24)

Turning In
The Correct Direction

Most people underestimate the importance of having a dog turn in the correct direction when given the hand signal to go *back*. Yet, it's true that when a dog turns to the left as it spins to go *back* it is likely to run back on a line slightly to the left of where you want it and to veer off slightly to the right if it turns to the right on the *back* cast.

Dog's have a natural tendency to turn in one direction or another, just as we have right- or left-handed tendencies, and the dog's turning tendency will become a habit if allowed to develop.

Jim Dobbs overcomes these tendencies in dogs he trains by encouraging them to spin in whichever direction he indicates by using his own right or left hand when giving *back* commands.

From the beginning of handling training Jim teaches that a right hand *back* means that the dog is to turn to the right as it spins to go *back* and a left hand *back* means spin to the left.

He teaches this by placing dummies slightly to the side of the direct line behind the dog. Standing very close in front of the seated dog, he gives the *back* command and gestures *back* with his right hand. He makes this an exaggerated gesture and, because of his close

[143]

position to the dog, the dog just naturally follows his hand and turns to the right. As it completes the turn it sights the dummy lying behind it and slightly to the right. Turning to the left is taught the same way, using the left hand and placing the dummy slightly to the *left* behind the dog.

The ability to make the dog turn to the right or left is beneficial later when the dog is being handled at a distance where distractions such as wind, terrain or cover may pull the dog off line.

The trainer's ability to turn the dog towards or away from such distractions can be used to compensate for the dog's tendency to drift off the intended line.

"A dog has just so many whistles in him," Jim says, meaning that a dog's response to hand signals diminishes as the number of handling corrections increases. "Anything you can do to get the dog into the right vicinity by *lining* it will improve the dog's success rate. Being able to make it turn to right or left improves the dog's *lining* accuracy and is therefore important."

(25)

Handling In Water

Once your dog is handling capably on land, it is time to move the same lessons to water. In the water everything happens in slow motion and is easier to control.

The first thing the dog must learn is to go *back* into the water on command. Start by working directly at the water's edge. Have the dog sit beside you so that your legs block it from escaping on your side. Put some sort of barrier on the other side of the dog to block it in that direction. (An overturned boat or a folding chair works well.) Then give the dog the *back* command and just as the dog enters the water, throw a dummy out beyond it to pull it on out. Repeat this until the dog anticipates that the dummy will be thrown and enters the water fast in order to be out there when it comes down.

Next the dog must learn to turn towards you and tread water when you blow the *sit whistle*. This is taught exactly as you taught the sit whistle on land. Use a combination of the single whistle blast and the verbal command "*sit*" to get the message through when you first start out. Then drop the verbal command and proceed using the

[145]

When teaching the dog to take hand signals while swimming, begin with short swims to visible dummies, then gradually lengthen the distance the dog must swim.

whistle alone once the dog learns to face you and tread water when the command is received.

Don't make the dog tread water long. When it turns and faces you give it a strong hand signal and a verbal *over* and throw a dummy so that it splashes into the water to the right or left of the dog. After a few of these are accomplished correctly, plant a dummy in plain sight on the side of the pond. Then send the dog into the water with a *back*, stop it with the *sit whistle* and give it an *over* to the visible dummy. Practice this on the right and then on the left. Eventually you can place dummies on the right and left and then send the dog whichever way you command. Keep the dummies in plain sight until the dog gets good at taking hand signals in the water, then start lengthening the distances.

Eventually you will be starting the dog some distance back from the water, sending it to enter the water on a *back*, stopping it in the water with the *sit whistle* and then giving the dog a hand signal and verbal command to go *back* or *over* to floating dummies fifty or sixty yards away. When the dog veers off line, stop it with the *sit whistle* and redirect it. If the dog is having trouble with this, shorten the distance until it is doing it right every time and then gradually increase the distance again.

Use of the Electronic Collar

Once the dog is adept at taking hand signals in the water, it's speed of entry and the crispness of it's response to hand signals can be increased by employing the variable intensity electronic training collar. With the receiver set at the lowest level to which the dog responds, you press the button as you give the *back* command and release it the instant the dog hits the water. The dog will learn that

The electronic training collar can be used to speed up a dog's water entry when sent for blind retrieves and also to illicit crisp responses to handling commands on land or water.

There's a joke about this Lab. His owner says he really doesn't like the water and trying to get most of the job done without getting his feet wet.

it can turn off the stimulation by running directly into the water and will speed up its entry. Likewise, if you press the button as you give the *over* command and release it as the dog turns in the proper direction, the dog learns that a crisp response turns the stimulation off. As the dog's crispness increases, stop using the stimulation altogether and let the dog see that it can avoid the stimulation by responding instantly.

(26)

Blind Retrieves
On Water

Getting a dog to go into the water to retrieve an object it did not see fall is often a problem. Many dogs get stuck at the water's edge and just don't know what to do.

Jim Dobbs of Marysville, California has a nice way for overcoming this problem. When he wants a young dog to cross a pond to retrieve a dummy planted on the other side, Jim uses the dog's natural tendency to backtrail as the motivating force.

He walks to the opposite side of the pond with the dog at heel and when he reaches the desired spot he puts the dog on sit at the water's edge and drops a dummy three or four feet behind the dog. Then Jim leaves the dog sitting there while he walks back around the pond to his original position. Once in position, Jim calls the dog and blows the *come in* whistle. He works from a point directly opposite the dog so that the dog will not tend to run the bank around the edge of the pond but will just swim straight towards him. This establishes the line in the dog's mind.

Jim calls the dog all the way to him across the water and then has it sit beside him. Now, when he sends the dog *back* to the dummy he left on the opposite shore, the dog will be recovering exactly the

Dogs will naturally follow their own backtrails. Jim Dobbs uses this to teach dogs to go back across water on blind retrieves. He will call this dog to him, then send it back on its own backtrail to a dummy planted behind where the dog is now sitting.

line on which it just swam across and it's natural tendency to backtrail will overcome it's earlier hesitation to go *back* on a "cold" water blind.

"It's just the dog's nature," Jim explains. "A dog that will not go *back* into water on a 'cold' blind will almost always go into the water on it's own backtrail. If it always finds a dummy at the end of it's swim, the dog's trust in your hand is deepened and after enough of these successes it will lose it's hesitation to go into the water on a 'cold' blind altogether."

This tendency to take its own backtrail can be used in lining practice on dry land, too, in making the transition from memory blinds to "cold" blinds.

(27)

Memory Blinds

Memory blinds, or pattern blinds as they are also called, are used to teach the dog to trust your hand signals and prove to him that there is *always* something to be retrieved out on the line you indicate with your hand.

Memory blinds are always planted in the same place so that the dog gets to know where to go to find the dummy. Instead of planting the dummy farther and farther away, you move farther and farther back from the spot where the dummy is always planted, thus causing the dog to run a longer distance on the line you give it with your hand without having to cross old scent.

The benefit of having a few memory blinds is that you can go back to them whenever the dog seems to be losing it's trust in your hand and not following the line you give it far enough. It's an easy way of extending the distance your dog will run on the line you indicate and once you have established the dog's confidence in you by giving it a few easy memory blinds, the dog will be more willing to trust your hand and extend its outrun on blind retrieves in unknown places.

When planting memory blinds always place the dummies in spots

When setting up lining drills, place dummy piles at the far end of your training field. Then, as the dog's proficiency increases, you can keep backing up to increase the distance the dog must run to reach "memory blind" locations.

[154]

at the far end of your training area. That way you can always place the dummies in the same places and can extend the distance the dog will have to go by gradually moving the starting line back towards the end where you normally enter the training area. You will eventually be able to use the full length of your training field and still put the dummies in the same place.

It's a good idea to mark the spots where the dummies are planted with something you can see so that you always give the dog precise lines to the right spot. A thin stick tipped with a piece of bright orange tape and driven into the ground at each spot where memory blinds are always planted will give you something to look at when you line the dog up.

Start by sending the dog from short distances and then keep backing up in subsequent lessons so that the dog has to run farther each time to reach the spot where the dummies always are. Once the dog learns that the dummies are always where they were last time he will run straight lines to those spots from very long distances. You can use memory blinds to refine the dog's ability to understand which line you want it to run. The dog learns to follow your hand precisely. It already knows where the dummies are, so the dog is concentrating completely on which dummy you want picked up.

When you get into trouble lining the dog in new places, you will always have the memory blinds to come back to. Once the memory blinds are imprinted in the dog's mind they will provide an everlasting exercise which will be useful to remind the dog to trust the line you indicate with your hand and follow it with absolute confidence that there will be a dummy there to retrieve.

(28)

Orange And White Dummies — When To Use Which

Since dogs see only in black and white, orange is a color they see as grey. Orange dummies, therefore, are to be used when you want the dog to have to use it's nose to find the dummy. Use orange when you are planting blinds to which you intend to send the dog either by lining or by hand signals. The dog will be forced to rely on your directions and its nose to find the dummy since it will not be able to see it from any appreciable distance. On the other hand, because the dummy is really orange and *not* grey, you'll be able to see it easily if you have to find it yourself.

White dummies are for use in marking and at any other time when you want to give the dog the advantage of an easily visible find. Use white in training exercises where you want the dog to use its eyes. When lining the dog to distant blinds you might want to use white dummies so that it will see them just at the time its outrun begins to peter out.

There are many training exercises which use a mix of orange and white dummies such as when you are refining a dog's lining skills. In that case you might line the dog between a pair of closer unseen orange dummies to a visible distant white one and then line it to the unseen orange ones. This will give the dog the advantage of visibility on the long run and make it trust in your hand and its nose to find the closer ones.

Remember, white is for sight, orange for nose.

(29)

Adding Realism: Birds And Guns

Dog training is a matter of teaching the dog the meaning of a command and then gradually increasing the level of distraction under which the dog will still respond to the command. A dog that is steady when dummies are thrown, will probably break when a pigeon is shot in front of it. Once it is steadied to thrown pigeons it will probably still break the first time you shoot a duck over it.

A dog used for hunting must be worked on birds before it can become an advanced performer. But don't let that make you hurry the time when birds are to be used. First train your dog using dummies. Get the commands down pat so that the dog always responds quickly and correctly. Then progress to using dummies combined with gunfire. When birds are introduced the level of distraction goes up considerably, so remember to progress in small steps. Start with dead frozen pigeons, then wing-clipped live pigeons and finally shackled ducks with gunfire added at each stage after the dog has become accustomed to the type of bird in use.

When you train the dog first on dummies and later on birds, you can always go back to dummy work to straighten out problems that arise later. Dogs that get too many birds too early become bored with

Hunting retrievers should be trained on dummies, then given work on birds after they have learned their lessons. If problems occur you can go back to dummy work to straighten them out.

work on dummies and you lose the ability to bring them back to basic training when you're in trouble.

Use birds for times when you want to increase excitement and raise the distraction level at which the dog will respond correctly.

Use live birds in training when you want to raise the excitement level and increase the level of distraction. Don't use birds until after the dog has learned his lessons on dummies.

(30)

Pigeons:
When And How

There is nothing like the flashy, clattering flight of a live pigeon to awaken birdy interest in your retriever. Pigeons help you to make training fun for your pupil, they are perfect for introducing your young dog to feathers, for establishing gentle-mouthed retrieves, for bringing out better marking ability and for teaching young dogs to hunt bird scent.

Joe Riser of Madison, Georgia, the outstanding retriever trainer who won the National Championship in 1966 and 1969 with Whygin's Cork Coot (and only narrowly missed the 1970 crown) uses live pigeons in almost ever facet of his training program.

Using live pigeons Joe Riser gets faster deliveries from his dogs. Pigeons enable him to put more excitement into his training program. Young dogs and veterans alike get loads of pigeon work. He uses them in simulated duck hunting and dove hunting situations and in developing a ground pattern in retrievers that are to be used for hunting upland game.

Pigeons are the least expensive live bird you can buy and keep for dog training. They have a heavy scent that attracts dogs and they are exciting fliers that keep dogs wound up tight during training sessions.

[163]

This inexpensive pigeon harness from T.E. Scott Dog Supplies, 10329 Rockville Rd., Indianapolis, Ind. 46234, is perfect for shackling homing pigeons for retrieving practice.

Riser prevents hard mouthed retrieves in his dogs by introducing pups to feathers early. For this he uses a dead pigeon which has been refrigerated over night. The refrigeration stiffens the bird and makes it easy for the pup to pick it up with a firm body hold. Refrigerated dead pigeons still have plenty of scent but are not bloody and warm. Thus dogs are less likely to clamp down hard on the bird. If the dog does tend to chomp on the bird, Riser pinches the dogs lip over his canine teeth, then pops the bird back in the dog's mouth and closes his jaws lightly over the dead bird. This lesson, repeated as often as necessary, is enough to discourage most retrievers from developing a hard mouth habit.

The most common fault among retrievers that are used for hunting is that they are not steady in the blind. When the gun goes off they're off, flaring any other birds that might be coming in, causing the shooter a moment of exasperation which usually makes him miss his second shot, and failing to mark the falls of any other birds that might come down after the first one hit the water.

To get steadiness in the blind, the retriever trainer must give his dog consistent schooling in practice training sessions. This means live birds, and pigeons are perfect.

Joe Riser sets up a mock blind and has his assistant throw live wing-clipped pigeons from a nearby location. Riser stays in the blind with the dog and enforces steadiness. Each time a pigeon is flighted he fires a blank pistol or shotgun popper, but he's right there with the dog, preventing the dog from breaking. When the bird is down and its fall has been marked by the dog, Riser sends him for the retrieve.

Any hunter who uses a retriever should be able to find a companion to throw birds and thereby duplicate this training process. Consistent repitition of this lesson will produce a retriever that is steady to shot in actual hunting situations. The dog learns that he must never leave the blind until he is sent.

As the dog's ability develops Riser actually kills pigeons in front of the dog, demanding steadiness and working up to double and triple retrieves. However, if you have prevented your retriever from developing a hard mouth, a few clipped-wing pigeons can be kept in a small pen and used day after day in training sessions.

Merely pull out or cut off the primary feathers from one wing only. This does not injure the pigeon but produces a bird that flies like mad but can't go anywhere. Grasping the bird by the base of the wings, pitch it underhand into the wind. The bird will stay airborne for up to a hundred yards, but its flight will describe a long tapering decline and it won't be able to fly from where it lands.

The exciting flight and long interesting fall really gives a dog something to study. He'll learn to mark the fall more precisely because of his added interest. That fact that there is a real bird out there with real bird scent speeds up the dog's pace and teaches him to use his nose to find the bird when his eyes have taken him close to the fall. He'll learn naturally to swing to the downwind side of the fall and to trail runners.

Working your dog out of a blind on wing-clipped pigeons is the most controlled, yet natural, simulation of a duck hunt you and your dog can devise for off season practice sessions. It's also the surest way to give your dog the repetitive lessons which will insure his steadiness in the blind come duck season.

Joe Riser also sets up simulated dove hunts and works the retrievers from hedgerow blinds on wing-clipped pigeons that are thrown from various points around an open field.

When a dog is steady in such situations a good "pressure test" is to release and shoot birds directly in front of him. Riser constantly tests steadiness, tempting the dog in every conceivable way to break, and demanding that the dog stay put until sent for the retrieve.

When Riser gets a retriever in for upland gundog training, he uses pigeons to develop the dog's hunting pattern.

Wing-clipped pigeons are released in scattered locations through typical pheasant cover. The birds are allowed time to walk around and leave some scent before the dog is released. Then, by working

Working dogs on wing-clipped pigeons provides a real test of the dog's steadiness. The same birds can be used repeatedly if the dogs have gentle mouths and blank cartridges are used.

Homing pigeons provide a plentiful supply of birds which can be used repeatedly in upland training. They fly home when released. Plans and parts for this handy backyard pigeon house are available from T.E. Scott Dog Supplies, 10329 Rockville Rd., Indianapolis, Ind. 46234.

the dog in a quartering pattern, Riser gets him into the birdy spots and the dog soon learns to hunt for bird scent and to cut back and forth in front of the gun.

Consistent work with guns going off and birds in the air is necessary if your retriever is to perform properly in actual hunting situations. No amount of work with dummies will suffice, although dummies are fine for learning basics. Before your dog will retrieve game properly and sit steadily in the blind when guns start going off and birds are coming down, he must be worked on live birds. There's a lot of difference between a blank pistol and falling dummy and the boom of a shotgun and a real bird tumbling out of the sky. Your dog must be prepared for the ultimate pressure.

Even after a lot of pigeon work the dog is likely to be put off the first time he encounters the different scent and larger size and weight of a duck or pheasant. For this reason it is important to give him some experience on the actual bird he will be retrieving before hunting season starts. If he has had plenty of pigeon work, however, his introduction to heavier game will be much easier to accomplish. Joe Riser goes from pigeon work into training with shackled ducks and pheasants and finally kills liberated ducks and pheasants in front of the dogs.

If that is too much of a production for the average hunting dog owner, you must at least work the dog on thrown dead game before expecting proper handling of ducks and pheasants in the field.

(31)

Keeping A Bird Supply

To really steady a retriever, you have to kill birds in front of it. Birds are necessary for training the retriever for upland hunting, too. Having a ready supply of birds is helpful whenever your training sessions need sparking up. Sometimes dummies get tiresome.

The best birds to use for gundog training are feral pigeons which you can either buy inexpensively from trappers or trap yourself.

There are a lot of pigeon traps offered for sale in dog supply catalogs, but most of them are not very efficient at holding pigeons. At this writing, the only pigeon trap that I've seen advertised that really works is one sold by T.E. Scott Dog Supplies, 10429 Rockville Road, Indianapolis, Ind. 46234.

The Scott trap is designed like the traps used by commercial pigeon trappers. It features one-piece entry gates which are recessed away from the sides of the cage to prevent trapped birds from finding the way out. I've tested this trap as well as others, and this is the one that holds birds best.

Wherever you see big flocks of pigeons you will find people who would like to have them removed. They dirty hay and grain in farmers' barns and around grain elevators and mess up window

Feral pigeons provide a plentiful bird supply and can be trapped on building roofs, around grain elevators and in old barns.

ledges and buildings roofs in town. Getting permission to trap pigeons for dog training is never hard.

Bait your trap with cracked corn, putting a pile in the middle of the trap and sprinkling a little around the outside to give the birds an easy start. They'll find their way into the trap each morning and should be removed each afternoon.

Pigeons can be kept in a simple wire pen with a roof over one end and flat boards mounted up high under the roof for roosting.

Keep cracked corn, gravel and fresh water before them and the birds will thrive.

Pigeons are strong fliers and make a loud flapping noise when they take off. This provides the kind of temptation that makes dogs break and gives you the opportunity to correct them and enforce steadiness to flush and shot.

(32)

The Electronic Bird Boy

If you could hire a person to throw birds or dummies for you during gundog training sessions and that person was absolutely reliable, ready to work whenever you needed, dependable in throwing the bird at the instant you required and never argued with you regarding training techniques, how much would a helper like that be worth?

You're probably thinking that people like that don't exist and can't be hired at any price, and you may be right.

Well, a little family enterprise in Washington state has developed and is now marketing an electronic bird and dummy thrower which is the space age answer to hiring dog training assistants. The Wag-Ag (short for Wagner Agricultural) Co., consisting of Larry Wagner and his wife Penny, produces an electronic releaser that is capable of throwing foot-long dog training bumpers 25 feet high. It also has a device which fires a .22 blank when the bumper is thrown if a shot is desired. Dog trainers can pay for a set of these releasers out of the savings afforded by not hiring less reliable human assistants.

The reliability of the Wag-Ag releaser is absolutely guaranteed. This thing works when you want it to. Aside from its extra size and power, the difference between the Wag-Ag and other electronic releasers is that this one has no moving parts to rust or get sticky with dirt. It also does *not* have rechargeable batteries. Instead, the Wag-Ag releaser works off a set of regular alkaline flashlight batteries that are available everywhere. There will never be a time when you find the releaser has to be recharged for several hours before you can use it. Just keep extra low-cost batteries on hand. When the batteries get low there is a warning light that tells you to put new batteries in. Battery life is extra long due to the very low amperage used to trigger the releaser.

This is the first electronic releaser that is built large enough and strong enough to throw heavy-duty training bumpers and birds up to the weight of full-grown pheasants and ducks. It's springs are powerful enough to throw a large-size dummy 25 feet straight up or farther if a folding leg is extended to angle the throw to the side.

Penny Wagner is a professional trainer of retrievers and pointing dogs and her husband, Larry, is an electronics engineer. Between the two of them they have full knowledge of what dog trainers need

The Wag-Ag electronic bird releaser can be used in place of a bird boy. It will throw a dummy or a gamebird every time at the touch of a radio button and will operate several hundred yards from the transmitter.

The electronic bird releaser is useful in training dogs to stop on flush and shot as well as for throwing distant marks when you are working alone. This unit will throw a full-size dummy more than 25 feet in the air and fires a .22 blank cartridge if desired.

and how to produce a foolproof bird thrower that does not fail in the field.

Other releasers use an electronically stimulated solenoid to open the latch on a spring-loaded release trap. In such models a large amount of electricity is required to trigger a solenoid strong enough to push the latch open. A solenoid is a little gismo that pushes out a thrusting rod when it is electronically triggered. When your car won't start in the winter it's usually because the solenoid sticks and you run your battery down trying to make it release. Solenoids are remarkable in their ability to fail when needed.

The transmitter which is used to trigger the releaser is a small box the size of a cigarette pack with a short extending antenna. With the antenna extended the transmitter will set off the releaser up to a quarter mile away. As additional release traps are purchased extra buttons can be added to the original transmitter, enabling those who use the device to operate up to four release traps individually from one another for multiple marks.

Marking Practice

Many retriver trainers use electronic releasers to throw birds or dummies at long distances for marking practice. Some trainers tape the transmitter to the forend of a shotgun. They swing the gun and fire a shot in the direction of the releaser and simultaneously trigger the radio transmitter causing the bird or dummy to be thrown in the distance right where the gun is pointed. The exercise is great for teaching dogs to mark off the end of the gun barrel. Several releasers can be placed in separate locations to create multiple marks.

The Wag-Ag releaser can be loaded and set to fire a .22 blank when the bird or dummy is thrown. This will help get the dog looking in the right direction to see the mark.

Releasers are also used to extend the distance dogs will run out in a straight line when sent from your side to make blind retrieves. You send the dog out with a hand signal and the command "back!" in the direction of the hidden releaser. Let the dog run as far as it will on the intended line, but when the dog's run starts to peter out and you know it is about to veer off-line, fire the releaser and suddenly the dog will see the dummy in the air straight on ahead and will be motivated to continue on the line you gave him. With

In *Stop To Flush* training, *the releaser is triggered as the dog approaches. Simultaneously, the sit command is given and the dog is either stopped with a jerk on the dragging checkcord, or by electronic stimulation. When the dog sits instantly at the "flush" it is given the reward of a retrieve.*

[175]

practice this exercise will cause the dog to extend the distance that it will run out on your command without wobbling off-line. Again, the .22 blank can be loaded and fired with the throw if the dog needs the extra help to make sure it sees the bird or dummy.

Sit On Flush

Later the same exercise can be used to teach the dog to sit when a bird is flushed or a gun is fired. Working at a short distance with the dog on a checkcord you walk toward the releaser but when you trigger the throw, you jerk the dog back and order it to sit. After a moment's delay, send the dog to retrieve the object thrown. With practice the dog will learn to anticipate that it will be ordered to sit when the flush occurs. Once this is understood, you can drop the verbal command and simply jerk the dog back with the checkcord when release occurs, reminding it to sit. With enough practice the dog will learn to sit automatically without a reminder when a bird or dummy is thrown.

Now you begin to lengthen the distance between the dog and the releaser, always insisting upon an instantaneous sit when the flush occurs. If the dog begins to get sloppy as the distance is increased, you'll have to shorten the distance again until the dog becomes precise. Finally, you begin to increase the distance between yourself and the dog. Have the dog quartering ahead of you when you trigger the release. He must sit when the flush occurs without hearing the command. By now the sight and sound of the flush has *become* the command to sit. Those who have electronic training collars will find them useful once the dog has been checkcord-taught to sit at the flush. The electronic collar gives the added ability to remind the dog to sit at the flush without uttering a verbal command.

Sitting at the Shot

Once the dog is reliable at sitting whenever a flush occurs, start loading the releaser with a .22 blank plus the dummy or bird. Now you will be teaching the dog to sit upon hearing a shot as well. Once the dog gets the idea you can mix things up. Make him stop to a flush one time and to a shot the next. Practice makes perfect and the dog will become increasingly reliable as you continue these lessons. The aim is to gradually increase the level of distraction at which your dog will reliably sit when it hears a gun fired or witnesses a flush.

The release trap is also useful for teaching the dog to take hand signals and extend the distance it will run when given "overs" and "backs." Once a dog has begun to understand your hand signals and will run out in the direction you indicate, you can extend the distance he will continue on that line by triggering the release of a dummy or bird up ahead when the dog is running in the right direction. Once it learns to expect something in that direction, no matter how far it may have to run out, the distance you can send the dog with signals will increase.

Tracking Practice

For teaching tracking you can trigger the release of a wing-shackled bird. Delay sending the dog and give the bird time to run off away from where the dog saw it thrown. When you do send the dog it will run to the spot where it marked the fall, but will have to use its nose and track the runner down to complete the retrieve.

(33)

Stop To Flush
(Without Electronics)

A retriever that is used for upland bird hunting should be taught to stop when a bird is flushed or a shot is fired. Likewise, the retriever that is used only for waterfowl hunting will be able to perform more reliably if it is taught to stop when a bird flushes or flies in when the dog is out of the blind making a retrieve, or when a shot is fired. It's more than just good manners; a dog that stops to the flush is better able to mark what happens to the bird. The dog that stops when a shot is fired has a better chance of marking the fall of whatever is being shot at.

Stop to flush is taught by making the sight or sound of a bird flushing or a shot being fired the same as a command to stop.

With your dog on a leash, and a blank pistol in hand, walk towards a planted bird. When the bird is flushed fire a shot and simultaneously jerk the dog back. Don't say anything, just jerk him back and make him stop. Repeat this several times each day, always jerking the dog back to prevent it from chasing when the bird is flushed and the shot is fired.

When the dog begins to anticipate the jerk and stops automatically when the bird is flushed and the shot fired, you're ready to begin

When a shot is fired the well trained hunting retriever sits instantly, marks the falling bird and awaits his handler's instructions.

increasing the distance between you and the dog when the bird is flushed.

Use a long checkcord and repeat the lesson only this time, instead of having the dog at your side when you flush and shoot, let the dog be forging ahead on the checkcord.

If you don't have an electronic bird releaser you can accomplish the same thing by carrying a live pigeon in your pocket and tossing it out in plain view of the dog and firing a shot as it flies away. Use the checkcord to jerk the dog to a stop each time until the dog stops on its own whenever you fly a bird or shoot.

The test comes when you take the checkcord off the dog. If you have an electronic training collar, now is the time to use it. The dog knows that it should stop to the flush or a shot, so you can use the electronic collar to enforce stopping.

If you do not have an electronic collar you will have to continue training with the checkcord longer, jerking the dog back whenever you flush a bird or shoot until it becomes automatic to the dog.

Some stubborn dogs may need more force. A chainlink spike collar causes pain when the checkcord is jerked and may be required for some dogs. Persistence and timing will eventually win out.

[180]

(34)

Upland Training For Retrievers

No more than thirty years ago, teaching a Labrador, Golden or Chesapeake retriever to quarter ahead of the gun seeking and flushing upland gamebirds was unusual. The retriever breeds' traditional duties had been two-fold: to excel in marking and retrieving fallen waterfowl and to be used as "non-slip" retrievers which walked at the gunners' heels waiting to be sent to retrieve upland birds shot over pointing dogs.

In days when there were fewer hunters, more game, larger bag limits and longer seasons, it made more sense to develop such specialists. But times have changed considerably. There is no spring shooting season now. Bag limits have dwindled and fall seasons have grown shorter. The hunter today must be versatile and so must his dog. He may hunt for ducks and pheasants in the same day, and he wants one dog that can assist him in both pursuits.

Increasingly since World War II, the old traditions which grew from the development of specialized breeds are being cast aside. It is common now to train pointing dogs to retrieve their own birds. Likewise, the retrieving breeds are becoming more versatile as more owners train them to quarter and seek upland game birds and to flush them for the gun before being called upon to perform their retrieving specialty.

As their versatility has grown the retriever breeds today come closer than ever before to meeting the requirements of the one-dog hunter whose desire it is to keep a single dog that "does it all" — retrieves ducks from cold and stormy waters, finds and routs out game birds within easy shotgun range, and happily keeps the family company the rest of the year.

In fact, the retriever owner today who has not taught his Lab or Golden or Chesapeake to hunt upland game is missing out on fully half of the sport and good times he can have with his dog.

Upland training, if it is begun at a logical spot in the retriever's training sequence, can be accomplished simply and quickly and goes hand in hand with training for water work. In fact, lots of water work is the best conditioner for a retriever that is to be used in the field as well.

Paul Genthner of Tealbrook Kennels, Monticello, Florida, has

A pretty Golden retriever delivers a pheasant that fell across water.

trained many retrievers for upland hunting. He feels that for effectiveness on pheasants in particular, a well-trained retriever is hard to beat.

"Take a shrewd old cock pheasant that wants to run rather than fly and finally holes up in the middle of the thick tangle of vines and briars," Paul says. "A well-trained upland retriever will work his track in a manner that lets the gunner stay close to the dog. He'll bust in and rout a bird out of the thickest and most briary cover — and he'll bring the bird back to you no matter where it falls."

A good retriever has guts. He's not afraid to smash through the heaviest cover. He's intelligent and he has a fine nose. He does not have the burning desire to run that a pointing dog has, therefore he is easier to control in the field.

Also, the dogs Paul Genthner has trained are easy to control in the field because he teaches them control first and delays their upland training until after the dog has been steadied and has had at least a month of work learning hand signals.

It is important that the dog has also been taught to stop on a whistle and to be steady to shot.

"If you start upland training before the dog has been taught hand signals, the dog will be more eager to hunt from the start, but if you can't control him, he'll be out there busting birds far out of range and you'd be better off walking the birds up yourself," Paul points out.

Not until a dog has his retrieving basics down pat, takes hand signals dependably, stops on a whistle, and is steady to shot, is he ready to begin having his hunting initiative developed.

For this job one of the most useful pieces of equipment is a bird releaser which will pop a live pigeon or pheasant into the air when triggered. You'll also need a supply of pigeons, quail or pheasants and a good-sized field with relatively open cover located well away from roads and other distractions.

Paul begins by scattering a few freshly-killed pigeons on a winding course across the prevailing wind. Then he starts down the course using the whistle and hand signals to get the dog working in a zig-zag back and forth pattern. He stops the dog and turns him whenever the dog goes out to 25 yards. That's the limit of a retriever's useful range. Birds that he routs out farther from the gun will be difficult or impossible targets.

[183]

In order that the trainer familiarize himself with exactly how far 25 yards really is, Paul suggests setting up white posts at measured 25-yard distances at several locations in the training area. For the trainer who may underestimate distances, the posts provide an accurate check on the dog's range and help develop a feel for what 25 yards really looks like.

Directing the dog down the course with hand signals, Paul is careful to take advantage of the wind direction. When he comes within range of a planted dead pigeon he signals the dog downwind of the bird rather than trying to put him right on it. This gets the dog using his nose.

In the beginning the retriever will be almost entirely dependent on the trainer, frequently stopping to look back and see where the boss wants him to go. But after he begins finding dead pigeons along the course, his interest will be awakened and he'll begin using his nose more and begin quartering on his own.

At this point the dog is still looking for dead birds to retrieve, however. Now comes the winder-upper.

The bird releaser with a live pigeon in it is set at the end of the course. The dog is directed downwind of the live bird, but this time, just as he winds the bird and starts for it, the releaser is triggered, popping the bird into flight ten feet or so ahead of the approaching dog. Simultaneously the trainer gives a blast on his whistle signalling the dog to stop, and carefully he kills the pigeon, dropping it in plain sight of the dog.

In the first session Paul lets the dog break and make the retrieve without waiting to be sent. At this point he is still trying to build the dog's excitement and interest in upland hunting. Later, once the interest has been awakened, he will use a checkcord and stop the dog on every flush, demanding that he mark the fallen bird and wait for a command to make the retrieve.

Paul uses scattered freshly-killed pigeons to develop the dog's quartering hunting pattern and desire to seek game. The flighted pigeons from the releaser add the excitement which gets the dog bouncing through the cover and quickly brings him to the point where range restriction must begin.

He moves the bird releaser to a new location each time it is used. Otherwise the dog would soon learn to make a beeline for the live bird rather than to hunt in a quartering pattern, finding and retrieving dead birds along the way.

As the dog's interest in hunting develops, keeping him within the 25-yard range becomes increasingly difficult.

At this point it is a good idea to attach a 50-foot drag line to the dog's collar. (Braided nylon water ski line slides through cover easily without tangling. A length of garden hose does the same thing but is heavier and helps slow a more aggressive dog.)

With the drag attached, the trainer continues working the dog on varying courses along which dead pigeons have been scattered. The trainer must be a fast stepper now. Whenever the dog fails to turn on the whistle, the trainer must grab up the checkcord and jerk the dog over backwards.

At this stage the dog must not be permitted to break when the bird flushes. Once he starts that habit he will go out behind one bird and then stay out there hunting and busting birds far out of shotgun range.

With careful, diligent training you can get your retriever to stop whenever a bird is flushed. Teach him first to stop on a whistle. Be sure you give a blast on the whistle every time a bird is popped out of the bird releaser. If the dog breaks and chases, jerk him over backwards with the checkcord. Then go to him, put him back where he was when the bird was flushed and make him stand still for a minute before sending him on.

This is important: if the dog breaks, the released pigeon should not be shot. You don't want to give the dog the reward of a retrieve when he has broken. Drag him back and make him think it over.

To make sure the dog will not break, Paul Genthner tempts the dog often. Once the dog has shown he will stop when the bird gets up, Paul tempts him to break by occasionally letting a bird fly away without a shot and at other times, intentionally missing the flighted bird.

At these times he immediately calls the dog to heel after the flush. This re-establishes the rapport between the dog and the man and gives the dog a break in time between the moment of the flush and the moment when he is sent on to hunt again.

If the dog has been taught to stop on a whistle and responds to hand signals before upland training begins, he will eventually learn to quarter and will be easier to prevent from breaking when the bird flushes.

A month or six weeks of this kind of training will get the average retriever really sharpened up for bird season.

As with most dog training problems, simulating the actual hunt as closely as possible during the training sessions is often a tough proposition. In early sessions you need pigeons. Later on the dog should be worked on pheasants or other real gamebirds before he can be expected to put it all together and act properly under actual hunting conditions.

In most states dog owners are permitted to train on wild birds with blank guns for at least the last month before hunting season opens. Most game preserves will also permit dog owners to train on actual game before the regular season opens.

One of the best reasons for using a retriever on upland game is for tracking down and retrieving wounded birds. Pheasants in particular are easy to hit but tough to kill. The dog needs practice in tracking down crippled runners.

For pre-season practice it's a good idea to drag a freshly-killed pheasant (or even a dummy swabbed with artificial game bird scent) through heavy cover, leaving the dead bird or dummy at the end of the track for the dog to find and bring back.

Consistent repetition of these training sequences will result in a controllable retriever that will not race about flushing birds out of range of your gun. But before you can hunt effectively with your retriever, you must teach yourself to read the dog's tail.

Since the retriver is a flushing dog, you don't have much time between the moment the dog finds a bird and the time when the bird is in the air. The dog's tail will give you the signal, but you've got to be watching for it.

When his tail begins working fast and stiff, watch out. Stay close to the dog and pick openings through which you can shoot if the cover is heavy. If the dog gets going too fast, you must stop him with the whistle before he gets too far ahead, but be prepared to do some fast stepping to keep even with the dog and give him a chance to work the bird out.

Retrievers are big-boned rugged animals that carry a lot more weight than the pointing breeds and are not built for running all day. For this reason the retriever works more slowly in the field. But even at his slower pace, he must be conditioned to get into the kind of shape that will enable him to quarter nicely for you for several hours at a time.

A good way to condition a retriever for upland work is to give him plenty of water work. Lots of swimming builds his muscle and his wind. Swimming also gives the dog plenty of exercise without encouraging him to run too fast to be controlled under field conditions. Furthermore, conditioning him with water work gives you the opportunity to continue his basic retrieving lessons at the same time that his upland abilities are being developed.

If upland training is delayed until after the dog has his basic retrieving lessons firmly implanted, there is no reason for his water work to suffer once upland hunting is begun. The average gundog of the retriever breeds can make an outstanding versatile hunting companion both in the blind and in the field if his upland hunting pattern is developed as a logical progression of lessons he has already learned as a straight retriever.

(35)

Mowed Paths Ease Dog Training

Among trainers of spaniels and retrievers, the lawnmower is becoming an essential piece of dog training equipment. (I can see you flashing mental pictures of dogs being chased by lawnmower-mounted disciplinarians, but that is not it at all).

Today more and more trainers are finding it advantageous to mow paths in particular patterns upon their training fields in order to help dogs understand lines of direction and establish boundaries within which they are to operate.

David Jones of Strong Kennels, Victoria, Texas is recognized nationally as an outstanding springer spaniel trainer whose innovative training techniques are consistently producing dogs that win big at major field trials and are also used regularly throughout the long Texas hunting season as gundogs.

The springers he trains are noted for their efficient ground covering quartering. Whether run into the wind, across the wind or in a downwind direction, his dogs sweep back and forth across the course in the pattern of a figure eight laid on its side. The dogs extend their sweep fully out to the recommended twenty yards either side of the handler, dipping somewhat closer to the handler

[189]

as they cross the front. Getting dogs to quarter in this pattern, back and forth across the front instead of forging out ahead is often the most difficult aspect of training gundogs, regardless of breed. Jones establishes this quartering pattern by using a very effective system of mowed paths.

On his training field David Jones has mowed paths in the shape of a long ladder. There are two parallel paths 40 yards apart extending about two hundred yards which are the sides of the ladder. Crosspaths, simulating the ladder rungs, are mowed across every twelve yards.

Jones does not start teaching his dogs the tight quartering patterns until after they have had one full season of actual hunting. "I want them to be very keen on hunting birds first," he says, noting that dogs that have a great desire to find birds are quicker to understand that they find more birds when they stick to the quartering pattern.

Jones starts dogs off using retrieving dummies, then graduates to dead pigeons and finally live birds. He has the dog sit in the middle of the course and lets it watch him drop dummies at both ends of the first path and another at the left end of the second path. He then sends the dog off to make retrieves, first to the dummy at the left end of the first crosspath, next for the one at the right end of the same path and then for the one at the left end of the second path.

"Long before any forward quartering is required you get the dog started fully extending his casts to the ends of the mowed crosspaths. Throughout the training he will alays find dummies or birds at the ends of the crosspaths. Unconsciously he will get into the habit of running out the full distance to each side of the handler rather than turning short and forging ahead."

Once the dog is accustomed to finding dummies that he has seen planted, Jones then begins to plant dummies along the edges of the course before the dog is brought out for training. Now the dog no longer knows where the dummies have been planted but searches for them in a quartering pattern with Jones using whistle and hand signals to swing the dog from side to side as he moves up the course searching for the hidden dummies.

"At this point the mowed paths give the dog reference points," Jones explains. "He learns that the sidebars mark the distance I want him to range either side of me. If he doesn't go out the full distance or overruns the sidebars by too much I get after him and the dog soon recognizes that the sidebars mark his boundaries. Likewise, the crosspaths measure the distance he is hunting ahead of me. I don't let him hunt out more than two crosspaths in front."

Consistency is one of the primary requirements of successful dog training. By working his dogs over the same course of mowed paths each day, always letting the dog find dummies at the ends of crosspaths and whistling the dogs back in when they hunt out much beyond the sidebars, Jones teaches a quartering pattern based on consistent reference lines that makes it easier for the dog to comprehend the lesson.

Once he gets the dog running out the full distance on each side expecting to find hidden dummies, Jones adds an element of further reward. Now he begins using freshly killed or frozen pigeons planted at random along the course at ends of crosspaths. He may plant a dummy, then two dead pigeons along the course and then work the dog over the full length of the course. When the dog really gets the hang of quartering and has adopted the habit of searching from side

Paths mowed in a ladder effect across a hayfield help springer spaniel trainer David Jones teach his dogs to quarter ahead of the gun when used for upland hunting. Birds are planted at the ends of the "ladder rungs" and the dogs establish a habit of sweeping back and forth twenty yards or so either side of the gunner.

[191]

to side without forging ahead, Jones adds the final reward, a live pigeon which is shot for the dog to retrieve after the flush.

At first Jones works the dogs always into the wind. As they get more adept at quartering he begins working them on a crosswind course. Eventually, because field trial judges are increasingly calling for downwind tests, he trains them for downwind work as well. In each case the pattern is the same and the dog is consistently encouraged to cover the full width of the course without going ahead more than the distance between two crosspaths.

Jones started using this technique for spaniel training after seeing other trainers using mowed paths as a method for teaching dogs to take straight lines when given hand signals. Retriever trainers commonly mow long straight paths across their training fields. Bisecting these paths at intervals are mowed crosspaths. Retrievers worked on mowed paths tend to run straight back along a path when sent in that direction by the handler. The handler then stops the dog with a whistle signal at an intersection and gives the dog an "over" to the right or left. Again, the dog will tend to run straight along the crosspath in the direction indicated rather than hooking or veering off the desired line. In this way retriever trainers use mowed paths to get dogs in the habit of running straight in the direction indicated by their hand signals.

"I saw the retriever guys doing that and I thought there must be some way I could use mowed paths to give my springers a better sense of reference when I teach quartering," Jones explains. He came up with the mowed ladder design and soon found that the paths not only made it easier for dogs to understand what was being asked of them, but it also largely eliminated the need for helpers.

Using the ladder design gives the dogs clearly recognized reference marks that tell them how far they should cast out to the sides before training. Use of the mowed ladder eliminates the need for two helpers and makes it possible to train alone, an important consideration for anyone who undertakes the training of a gundog.

Using the mowed paths every day it takes David Jones an average of two months to get a dog really quartering well. He usually plants five or six dummies or birds for each lesson and sometimes gives a dog two lessons a day. By the end of two months the dogs have the quartering pattern so deeply imprinted that they no longer need paths as reference marks and will continue quartering in the same pattern when taken hunting anywhere. In the future, if the dog begins to develop any sloppiness in his quartering pattern he can always be brought back to the mowed paths for brush-up lessons. Once a dog has been taught to quarter by this technique it retains an understanding of range based on the reference paths. Because of this it is easier for the dog to comprehend his error when corrected for ranging too far or not far enough.

Although David Jones developed this technique for working with springer spaniels, his innovative method is equally applicable in training other flushing breeds. In any situation where a dog is to be taught to turn within boundaries or to run in straight lines the use of mowed paths can be very effective.

(36)

Teaching Your Dog To Shake On Command

Do you like to have your dog shake water all over you after retrieving each duck? Neither do I, but I always accepted that as one of duck hunting's unpleasant aspects, just like being wet and cold and up too early.

Then I met professional trainer Jim Dobbs of Marysville, California and noticed that his dogs always delivered their ducks directly and didn't shake until they were told they could. Jim could train in water for hours and end up dry.

Here's how he does it.

"Given its own way the dog would come out of the water, lay down the duck and shake, right" Jim queried. "But you want the duck delivered without delay and you don't want the dog to shake until you're out of the way. So you trick the dog into thinking the delayed shake was really its own idea."

You start by meeting the dog at the water's edge and taking the bird from its mouth the minute it hits dry land. Then you step back and, just when the dog is going to shake anyway, you say "Shake," and then praise the dog for obeying even though the dog didn't realize it had done anything. Continue doing this for several water training sessions, always taking delivery before the dog has a chance to shake and then ordering it to shake just when it is about to anyway. Then start moving back a bit so that the dog now comes out of the water, and takes a few steps towards you before you take delivery. Again, accept delivery and then command it to shake when it's going to anyway.

In each water training session you must be consistent in showing the dog that it always gets a chance to shake, but that the delivery must be completed first.

Don't forget to praise the dog each time it shakes on command. It'll get the idea what "shake" means and begin to wait for the command. As its proficiency increases, move back farther from the water's edge until you are ten, twenty, thirty feet back. If the dog does stop on its way from the water to you, blow the "come in" whistle, clap your hands and run backwards to hurry the dog to you. Then take the dummy, step back and order the dog to "shake." If the dog fails and shakes before you tell it to, move closer to the water again and practice at a distance at which the dog always succeeds.

When the dog gets good at waiting for the command, you can begin to delay giving it slightly. Take delivery and move a few steps away from the dog before giving the command to shake. Eventually, you will be able to accept the delivery and then gesture for the dog to move a few steps away from you before you give the command. Dogs that are brought up this way right from the moment water work begins are very quick to learn to wait for the command before shaking. Dogs that have already started water work may take a little longer to get the idea, but will respond if you are consistent in adhering to this procedure every time from now on.

This is a training achievement you and your duck hunting friends will appreciate most on those cold mornings in a duck blind.

Hunting retrievers should be trained to shake on command after completing water retrieves. You and your companions will all be drier and happier at the end of every hunt if you haven't had to put up with wet dog showers all day.

(37)

Your Responsibility To Your Retriever

The level of competence to which a good retriever can be trained is constantly being pushed higher. But something you might not have thought about is that the handler's responsibility to his dog increases with the dog's level of training.

The dog's achievement level grows according to its trust in its handler. The dog that *lines* out straight for a couple of hundred yards without stopping does so because it knows from experience that its handler would not send it out unless there was something out there to retrieve. To reach the highest levels of achievement dogs have to overcome their natural cautions and trust their handler entirely. A dog that has been trained to this degree no longer has its own safety as its first priority and can willingly be sent into dangerous situations.

Consider for a moment the retrievers you see hit the water at top speed and arc out in a flying leap. True, it's spectacular to watch. But do you really want your hunting retriever to hit the water like that? What about submerged rocks and sunken logs? Dogs that leap like that have been trained in water where their handlers know there are no underwater dangers and run at field trials where someone has made sure the water entry places are safe. Can you guarantee your

[199]

dog a safe entry where you hunt? You'll be doing your hunting retriever a favor to practice in places where there *are* submerged obstacles so that it will learn from the start to make sane water entries.

And what about tides and river currents? It's all very well for retrievers to be sent for long swims in the safe ponds where you train and where field trials and hunting tests are run, but when you are hunting you must realize that there are times and places where your retriever should *not* be sent.

When we are hunting sea ducks off the coast of Maine in dead winter, for instance, we never send the dogs after cripples. It's too easy for a crippled bird to pull a dog so far offshore that it will not be able to make it back against the tide. We either kill the birds dead and then send the dog or we go after the cripple with a boat. Cripples on a big river can get your dog in trouble, too. They'll swim for the open water and pull the dog so far offshore that it may get swept far

Enthusiastic water entries are thrilling to watch and no one wants a dog that tiptoes into the water. But you have a responsibility to teach your dog that underwater obstacles can be dangerous. Don't encourage high arcing leaps into the water at a safe training area and then work him where danger may lurk beneath the surface. Better to work him in rough places from the beginning and let the dog learn to adjust its water entry to suit conditions.

Give the dog a break. When you're hunting in rough seas send the dog into the water from a place where it can land safely as Whistler is doing with an eider off the coast of Maine.

[201]

Whistler retrieving a surf scoter on a ledge off the coast of Maine. On the ocean we only send dogs to retrieve when the ducks are dead. Cripples can pull the dog so far offshore that it may not be able to swim back against the tide. Cripples are chased down by boat.

downstream before it can make a landing — and the land it reaches may be on the far side of the river. If the river is a mile wide, what next?

Your retriever will be able to stand the cold better than you will, but don't make it suffer unnecessarily. Swimming in frigid water lowers the dog's body temperature and reduces the time it can sit still in the blind.

Because your dog will go whenever you send it, it's your responsibility to put the dog only in situations which you know it can handle. Don't shoot from spots where the dog can't make safe retrieves unless you have a boat to use for backup. Consider what you are about to send the dog into before you send it. Sometimes you should walk the bank with the dog and send it to make the retrieve from a safer position. Even though your dog has been trained to make retrieves at incredible distances, there are times when it will be to your advantage to walk the dog near the vicinity of a fall and send it for a short retrieve that is not totally reliant on long distance handling skills. Your hunts will progress more pleasantly if you refrain from pushing your dog to the limit and, instead, help the dog do its job safely and with as little difficulty as possible.

(38)

What About Channel Blinds?

Channel blinds are a field trial gimmick designed to eliminate most of the dogs that are entered so that the judges can limit their evaluation to the few dogs that remain in competition. Channel blinds are totally useless from a hunter's standpoint and are only worth mentioning here as a reminder of the difference between field trial training and training a retriever for hunting.

In a channel blind the dog is required to swim the full length of a narrow channel of water to pick up a duck at the far end and is then required to re-enter the water and swim all the way back, regardless of the fact that the dog could have brought the duck back in a fraction of the time if it simply ran the bank. Bank-running is not permitted in field trials if it causes the dog to diverge from the straight line from the handler to the bird.

When you are hunting, forcing the dog to stay in the water in such situations makes no sense. Not only would bank-running get the duck in hand faster and reduce disruption of the hunt, but in cold weather the dog will be able to stay in the duck blind longer if it is not subjected to unnecessary swimming.

Channel blinds are strictly a demonstration of a dog's training and in that respect they are responsible for more brutal punishment than any other retriever test. Since it is against the dog's nature to remain in the water when it can do its job faster on its feet, training for channel blinds requires that dogs be shocked, shot with pellet guns and slingshots, zapped with cattle prods and generally abused whenever they try to leave the water to complete the retrieve the obvious best way.

Channel blinds have no validity in hunting retriever tests.

(39)

Making Practice Seem Real

When your dog goes hunting it will be worked from a blind or duck boat, with a big spread of decoys out front and probably several people blowing duck calls and shooting when the birds approach. He'll be faced with situations that are much more distracting and tempting than he gets when you work him in a training field.

The way to get him ready for the pressure he will be facing when actually hunting is to make your training as similar to hunting as you possibly can. This means working him from a real blind or duck boat during training sessions.

Whenever possible, take your dog for a training session at one of your regular duck blinds or from your duck boat. Put out large numbers of decoys and bring along some friends to blow duck calls and shoot multiple shots as shackled ducks or dummies are thrown.

A dog that has been trained from a blind knows where his place is and how he is expected to behave during a real hunt.

Dogs that have worked through big spreads of decoys learn to avoid getting tangled in the strings. If you neglect that aspect

Once your dog has been gradually introduced to gunfire and becomes accustomed to the sound of shotguns, you should train with a 12 gauge shotgun and loud popper loads. Make training as similar to real hunting as you possibly can.

When you're hunting you will frequently shoot from a sitting position. Get your dog accustomed to this by sometimes shooting from a sitting position while training, too.

Be sure your training includes lots of practice runs through groups of decoys. The dog must learn to avoid getting tangled in the strings.

of training your dog will get tangled in the decoys every time you send him for a retrieve. You don't want that to happen when you're hunting.

(40)

Tracking Training

Too often retriever owners try to handle their dogs to every fall and don't give them the chance to hunt on their own. Remember, the dog is the one with the nose — let him use it.

When you have a bird down and the dog has marked the fall, send the dog quickly and when he reaches the vicinity of the fall, let the dog use its nose and hunt. Let him learn to use the wind to his advantage. Give him time to hunt thoroughly so that he develops a quartering hunting pattern. If he is having a hard time finding the bird it may be that the bird was crippled and has run off. If that's the case, you don't know where it is either, so don't attempt to handle. The dog must learn to find scent and trail it.

The only time to give the dog hand signals is when you know exactly where the bird is and the dog has gotten out of the right vicinity.

Your dog will become a good tracker if he has been given the chance to learn how. You can help develop this ability by adding tracking training to your repetoire.

Spray a dummy with commercial duck or gamebird scent and drag it on a string from the edge of a field into heavy cover. Start with

Learning to track down cripples is an important part of the hunting retriever's job. Scent trails can be laid by dragging a scented dummy or a dead bird.

short drags and lengthen the distance farther and farther as the dog gets the idea. This is the way foxhounds are trained and they will follow a track laid out this way for hours over several miles. Retrievers don't need mile-long tracks but can easily learn to handle trails that continue for as far as you feel like laying them. A twisting trail a couple of hundred yards long is enough to give your dog the confidence to seek a trail and follow it when it can't find a fallen bird.

Lay tracks from the edge of water into heavy cover, too.

Once the track is laid, give the dog a line to a spot just a few feet downwind of the point where the trail begins. Start with short trails and lengthen them day by day.

Don't lay a new track over an old one on the same day during early sessions, but later on, once the dog has become a proficient tracker, laying a new track over an old one will help the dog learn to differentiate between older scent and fresh, just as it will have to do in real hunting situations when several birds fall in the same area.

(41)

Daily Training Plans

When you go out to train, do just that. Don't just throw a few dummies for your dog and call it training. Have a plan in mind. Know what you are going to do. Many trainers make daily notes to remind themselves of areas where their dogs need special work so that they won't forget to devote emphasis to that area next time out. It's a good idea.

To help you get started with some training plans in mind, here are some sample sessions which get a broad amount of work covered in about fifteen minutes. Use these as examples; then make up your own game plans based on what your dog needs.

Pups under Six Months
Practice coming when called.
Practice sitting on command.
Practice heeling.
Four or five simple dummy retrieves on land.
Four or five simple retrieves on water.
Introduce gunfire at feeding time.

[213]

Pups Six Months to a Year
    Force breaking to retrieve.
    (No other lessons during this process.)

Force-broken Pups, Six Months to a Year
    Session A
    Introduce gunfire with retrieves.
    Lengthen distance of retrieves.
    Retrieves in high grass to require nose work.
    Retrieves in heavier cover.
    Practice sit to deliver.
    Practice whistle sit.
    Session B
    Water retrieves out of boat.
    Simple doubles on land, water.
    Whistle sit.
    Marking off gun barrel.
    Work from training box.
    Practice sit to deliver.

When you go out to train have a training plan in mind. Don't just go out and throw dummies and call it training.

Force-broken Dogs That Have Been Shot Over For One Hunting Season

Session A

Steadying to shot.

Memory Blinds

Hand signal - "back" - on land, water.

Session B

Steadying to shot.

Hand signals - "overs" - on land, water.

Lining drill - Wagon wheel.

Session C

Mixed overs and backs.

Memory blinds.

Wagon wheel drill on land.

Honoring other dogs.

Session D

Work from blind or boat with decoys.

Wagon wheel lining drill on water.

Mixed overs, backs on water.

Marking off gunbarrel.

Advanced Training, Polishing the Finished Product

Session A

Handling; cross pattern.

Lining to blinds.

Memory blinds on land.

Session B

Handling; cross pattern on water.

Lining drill across water.

Turning in correct direction.

Session C

Upland quartering.

Stop to flush, shot.

Tracking training.

Session D

Handling, double cross on land, water.

Lining across land, water.

Shake on command.

Memory blinds.

Make training sessions interesting by moving from one area of instruction to another. Give the dog three or four retrieves in one category, then move on to the next category and do three or four retrieves there. You'll find your dog will learn faster if he's not bored by doing the same thing over and over again. He'll start looking to you with an expression that tells you he wonders what you're going to ask him to do next. That interest makes training more fun for both of you and the dog will learn faster when he's eager.

(42)

Maintenance Training For Retrievers

Ask any professional dog trainer why hunting dogs go sour when they are home with their owners and you'll get one common answer: the owners fail to maintain the training which the dog has been given. It's like teaching a kid to read and then denying him access to books for a year and expecting his reading ability to stay high.

Maintenance training is the dog owner's responsibility once his pup comes home from school. If training is maintained by frequent reminder lessons, the dog will continue to give peak performances year after year. Let training slip and performance levels fall apart.

Retriever trainer Joe Riser of Madison, Georgia, has an outstanding reputation for bringing retrievers to peak performance levels and keeping them there. He works on the dog's memory. Through frequent repetition of lessons learned earlier, Riser keeps his dogs sharp.

That is where many hunting retriever owners fail. Whether they have trained their dogs themselves or had the job done by a pro, they fail to realize that training is a job that is never finished. Once a dog has learned to perform respectably, he must be continually reminded of his lessons through regular practice sessions.

[217]

Training is a never ending process. Once your dog has learned the necessary lessons you must give him frequent practice to keep his responses sharp.

Riser's maintenance techniques are inventive. He makes staying in school fun for the dog, never allowing training to become boring for either the dog or the trainer. Much of his maintenance training can be duplicated by any retriever owner either singly or with the help of a hunting buddy.

It is not hard to make a retriever steady to shot. But keeping him steady when the ducks are flying and guns are going off is a different matter entirely. Once he has broken on shot and gotten away with it, chances are that thereafter the dog will leave the blind the moment guns are raised to shoot. This is both disconcerting and dangerous.

To steady a retriever, Joe Riser attaches a strong 20 foot checkcord to the dog's choke collar and ties the end of the cord to a stout tree or post. Then he throws a live pigeon in front of the dog and fires a blank pistol. Without being sent to retrieve, the dog dashes out after the pigeon and when he hits the end of the line is flipped end for end. When the dog breaks, Riser says firmly, "NO!" After a few such lessons the dog has lost his eagerness to break.

Once the dog has proven his steadiness, Riser tests the dog's memory regularly. He tempts the dog to break by commanding "back" without putting his hand next to the dog's face. Dummies are thrown in front of the dog and pigeons are shot temptingly right in front of the dog. At no time is he permitted to leave the line without the combination of the verbal command and directional hand signal.

The retriever owner who similarly tests his dog's steadiness several times a week throughout the year will have a steady dog in the blind with him come duck season. The dog that breaks is the one that has not been reminded frequently that he may leave only when his master sends him with the combination of a verbal and hand signal.

A retriever's ability to take hand signals must be kept sharp once the dog has reached that degree of training. And don't let anyone convince you that hand signals are only for field trial retrievers.

A good maintenance technique which Joe Riser uses to keep well-trained retrievers on their toes involves the same use of an imaginary baseball diamond laid out in large dimensions and covered with knee-high grass. The distance across the diamond might be two hundred yards. A dummy is planted at each imaginary base.

[219]

Riser stands with the dog at home plate, giving him a line toward second base. He sends the dog "back," then stops him on a whistle and makes the dog sit approximately at the pitcher's mound. Then with hand signals and verbal commands he sends the dog "back" to second base, or "over" to first or third.

This little brush-up course, even if only used for ten minutes once a week, will keep a well-trained retriever in mind of what the hand signals and the verbal commands mean. Also it requires steadiness, and sitting on the whistle, as well as keeping the dog in practice on taking a line when sent from the trainer's side.

No fancy equipment or bird boys are needed in the simple procedure; anyone can give his retriever this necessary brush-up course without needing anything more than three dummies.

One good memory test is to walk along a tote road with your retriever and let him see you throw a dummy into the brush. Then walk back down the road with the dog at heel. When you have retreated a distance that you feel will challenge the dog, make him sit at your side, give him a line to the fall, and send him to make

Lining drills on land and water will result in more birds retrieved with the least amount of handling. A dog that will follow the line you send it out on until it finds a bird or is stopped by your whistle is the ultimate hunting retriever.

When you are hunting alone and have no means of enforcing steadiness if your dog should break, it's a good idea to tie the dog and prevent a breaking habit from getting started.

the retrieve. If he gets good at this, increase the distance and begin using the same method to get into widespread doubles and doubles in line. Present him with depth perception problems.

Riser keeps his dog's marking ability sharpened up by giving him frequent long retrieves on dummies or live game. A helper is sent out a hundred yards or more from the trainer and dog. When the trainer shoots, the helper throws a bird or dummy in the air. On long retrieves such as this only continuing practice enables the dog to perceive the distance to the fall and mark the spot accurately.

This game is played frequently and under differing circumstances. Varying wind directions teach the dog to swing downwind of the spot where the fall was marked.

"One thing you've got to remember," Riser says. "A good retriever likes his job; he's happy and eager. Remember to make training fun for him."

Riser starts every training session by letting all the dogs in his string out for a romp with the boss. He lets the dogs race around

No dog ever learned anything good from running loose without supervision. Keep your dog with you or in its kennel at all times and bad behavior patterns won't get started. Dogs crave human companionship, not unsupervised freedom.

[222]

him and throws handfuls of dummies into the water yelling "Okay! Okay!" as the dogs charge into the water and race for the dummies without anyone asking them to wait or be steady. For five minutes Riser plays with the dogs and asks nothing from them.

Then he blows the whistle and orders them to sit. The dogs' fannies hit the ground instantly. Playtime is over, school has begun. From then on it's all business, but the dogs have just had fun with their boss and they enter into the schooling session happy and eager to please him.

It's that refined sense of timing that Riser has which tells him when to play with his dogs, when and how to demand top performance and when to use discipline, that makes him an outstanding professional trainer.

But it is maintenance training that keeps his dogs at peak performance levels after their initial instruction is complete.

(43)

Training The Versatile Retriever

It had been calm when we were setting decoys at dawn along the Nebraska shoreline of Lewis and Clark Lake, but later the prairie wind came up out of the northwest, and soon big waves were battering our spread. Picking up the decoys was going to be a tough proposition for they had been set at the edge of deep water and now most were out of the reach of men in waders, and the wind-driven waves made it hard to manuever the duck boat.

"Just pick up the decoys we can reach easily," Ron Raynor told us. "Jake can get the rest for us."

Jake was Ron's big Chesapeake retriever and, sure enough, when Ron pointed to one of the outside decoys and told Jake to "fetch", the big dog hit the water and swam out and grabbed the decoy Ron had indicated. When he brought that decoy in, Ron pointed to another decoy that was beyond our reach and sent Jake after it.

"Field trialers tell me I shouldn't do this," Ron chuckled. "They say someday Jake is going to bring in a decoy instead of a duck at a field trial. In the meantime I sure do appreciate having this kind of service."

Ron Raynor is a professional gundog trainer and Chesapeake

retriever breeder from R. R. #1, South Sioux City, Nebraska, and his maverick training techniques are appealing to anyone who understands the situations that retrievers encounter under actual hunting conditions.

"To my way of thinking a retriever is supposed to retrieve anything I want him to bring back," Ron explained. "I train them to retrieve all sorts of things — pails, Thermos bottles, the rope on the bow of the duck boat, decoys — anything that may float away when we're actually out hunting in rough weather."

Several times that morning when the wind dragged a decoy into deep water where it began to float away, Ron sent Jake after the errant decoy and was saved from having to disrupt the hunt by chasing the decoy down with the boat.

At the end of the morning when Jake started helping out by bringing in the decoys, we couldn't reach without going over our waders, his versatile retrieving services were a real advantage.

"Retrievers are supposed to bring things back," Ron said. "Whoever said that ducks and geese and gamebirds were all they are supposed to retrieve for us?"

"I train my dogs to swim around the decoys when they are retrieving ducks so that they won't tangle in the decoy lines when completing the retrieve," Ron explained. "But at the end of the training session, I have the dogs swim out and bring the decoys in. They know the difference. Any dog that retrieves a decoy when he is sent for a duck simply hasn't been trained to handle both jobs."

Ron teaches his dogs to retrieve whatever he points out. He starts this at a young age as part of force training the dog. When a dog is sent to pick up a decoy, it must pick up the one Ron indicates, not just any decoy. "Dogs are very quick to learn to get the one you are pointing at," Ron says. "Once they have been worked this way for a while they know that the decoy you want is the one that's floating away. If they go after the wrong one, you simply say 'no' and give them a hand signal towards the one you want."

I've used my Chesapeake retriever Whistler unconventionally myself.

While hunting pheasants and quail in Kansas, I kept seeing fat cottontail rabbits scuttling out of our way. The pointing dogs were paying no attention to them, but the rabbits were moving away from the commotion made by the bird dogs passing through heavy cover.

Every thicket had rabbits, and the plump bunnies were easily visible skittering through the thick tangles. I didn't want to shoot rabbits in front of the bird dogs, and I didn't want to have to crawl into these awful thickets to pick up dead rabbits so I was passing them up. But I had *hassenfeffer* on my mind.

Unloading Whistler from the truck, I told the others to go on ahead with the bird dogs. I followed them about fifty yards behind with Whistler walking at heel. Next time a cottontail came slipping back through the thickstuff, running away from the bird dogs, I shot it and sent Whistler into the thicket to make the retrieve. Admittedly, she gave me an odd look when she discovered what I'd shot, but I said "fetch" and she picked it up and brought the bunny to my hand. From then on she was a rabbit retriever as well as a top-notch waterfowl and upland game picker-upper. I brought home a possession limit of fat, cornfed Kansas cottontails that Whistler had brought out of the briar thickets and we made some of the most succulent *hassenfeffers* you can imagine.

I told Ron Raynor that story and said, "Hell, I've got one Chesapeake I even take coon huntin' — he'll tree 'em and carry 'em back to the truck, both. . ."

Field trial retriever trainers wear white jackets while training and when handling dogs at field trials because the white jacket is extra visible and helps the dog see the handlers' hand signals from a distance. Ron Raynor wears camoflage instead.

"When I go hunting, I wear camoflage like every other duck hunter." Ron argues. "I don't want my dog to be looking around for some guy in a white coat so I train in camo, too. White coats for cryin' out loud!"

Raynor also teaches his dogs an unconventional two whistle system which simplifies handling retrievers to game the dogs did not see fall. "It's the same system sheep dog trainers use," he explains. "Two short beeps on a whistle means go left, one beep means go right. You can stop the dog with one long whistle blast and then send him in the direction you want without having to get out of the blind and wave your arms. It makes a great deal more sense in actual hunting conditions because it causes a lot less interruption of the hunt."

When our hunt on Lewis and Clark Lake was over and we all

gathered back at the pickup trucks, Raynor turned to Jake and said, "Want a beer, Jake?"

The big dog looked at him joyfully and wagged his tail.

"Yeah, I'd like one too," Raynor responded. "Get us a six pack." He pointed to a cooler in the back of the truck.

The Chesapeake nudged open the cooler and pulled out a six pack of Blue Ribbons and Raynor started passing them around.

"Nothing like a versatile retriever," he said.

"Jake, ole Buddy, now why dontcha slap some music on the tape deck and then get me out a cigar. . ."

(44)

How Far Do You Want To Take It

You now have the information you need to train a fine hunting retriever. How far you go in training will be a matter of interest and desire. Any dog that has been trained in basic obedience, force trained to retrieve gently to hand and will follow hand signals, has the education to be taken as far up the training ladder as you wish.

From now on it's a matter of adding distractions and diversions like multiple shots, multiple birds falling and birds being shot when the dog is coming in with a bird in its mouth. You can increase the distance your dog will follow a line or take hand signals by patiently adding distance bit by bit. You can add to the distraction level by sending the dog across patches of cover and bands of water to distant falls. It's only a matter of practice and expanding the dog's foundation of knowledge one step at a time.

A good hunting retriever is the best buddy you'll ever have. If you are fair with your dog, firm but not frightening, there is no limit to the enjoyment you will have together.

Happy hunting!

A good hunting retriever is the best pal you'll ever have. Be fair in what you ask it to do and train with firmness but not anger and there is no limit to the enjoyment you'll have together.

Index

[232]

Notes

Notes

Notes

Notes

Notes

Notes

Notes

Notes